An Inventory of Submerged Aquatic Vegetation and Hardened Shorelines for the Peconic Estuary, New York

by

Ralph W. Tiner, Herbert C. Bergquist, Denise Siraco, and Bobbi Jo McClain

U.S. Fish and Wildlife Service
Northeast Region
National Wetlands Inventory Program
300 Westgate Center Drive
Hadley, MA 01035

Prepared for the Peconic Estuary Program of the Suffolk County Department of Health Services, Office of Ecology, Riverhead, NY*

December 2003

*Note: This study was supported in part by the U.S. Environmental Protection Agency through assistance agreement #CE992002 to the Suffolk County Department of Health Services.

This report should be cited as: Tiner, R.W., H.C. Bergquist, D. Siraco, and B.J. McClain. 2003. An Inventory of Submerged Aquatic Vegetation and Hardened Shorelines for the Peconic Estuary, New York. U.S. Fish and Wildlife Service, Northeast Region, Hadley, MA. Prepared for the Peconic Estuary Program of the Suffolk County Department of Health Services, Office of Ecology, Riverhead, NY. 47 pp.

Executive Summary

The Peconic Estuary Program (PEP) is interested in the extent of eelgrass and other submerged aquatic vegetation and in documenting changes in the shorelines of the Peconic Estuary. The Suffolk County Department of Health Services' Office of Ecology provided funds to the U.S. Fish and Wildlife Service to gather geospatial information on submerged aquatic vegetation (SAV) and the extent of hardened shorelines and docks in the Peconic Estuary. The Service used conventional photointerpretation techniques to identify and map these features. This inventory delineated 1,339 beds of submerged aquatic beds totaling 3,539 acres in the Peconic Estuary. About 44 percent of the beds was represented by eelgrass. East Hampton was first-ranked among towns in SAV acreage and in eelgrass abundance. Eelgrass beds were also extensive in the towns of Shelter Island and Southold. Gardiners Island and Shelter Island critical natural resource (CNR) areas contained the most SAV acreage. Among the CNR areas, Shelter Island and Orient had the greatest acreage of eelgrass.

Almost 29 miles of hardened shorelines and nearly 9 miles of docks were mapped in the Peconic Estuary. Eighty-two percent of the hardened shorelines were bulkheads and seawalls. Southold had the greatest length of hardened shorelines, with 12.6 miles inventoried. It possessed almost twice the length of bulkheads and seawalls as Southampton, the second-ranked town in hardened shoreline coverage. Of the CNR areas, Northwest Harbor and Arshamonaque had more than two miles of hardened shores. Cow Neck, Cutchogue, Shelter Island, and Threemile/Accobonac Harbors each had more than one mile of hardened shorelines. Northwest Harbor had the greatest length of docks, with nearly one mile or 5,381 feet of these structures inventoried. Montauk and Cutchogue had more than 4,000 feet of docks.

Table of Contents

Introduction

Submerged aquatic vegetation (SAV) is an important coastal resource providing habitat for fish and shellfish and for stabilizing nearshore sediments, among other functions. Knowing the distribution and trends of this resource will aid coastal resource managers in their planning and management activities.

These managers are also interested in the learning about changes in the shoreline, especially due to the construction of hardened shorelines (e.g., bulkheads and seawalls). An inventory of hardened shorelines and physical barriers is the first step in assessing the impacts that these structures may have on local natural resources. This inventory will also serve as a baseline from which estimates can be made regarding the rate at which natural shorelines are being replaced by hard structures.

One of the many objectives of the Peconic Estuary Program (PEP) is to preserve and enhance the integrity of the ecosystems and natural resources present in the study area. PEP wanted geospatial information on SAV and hardened shorelines for coastal resource planning and management. The U.S. Fish and Wildlife Service (Service) has been mapping wetlands and deepwater habitats as part of its National Wetlands Inventory Program (NWI) since the mid-1970s.

The Suffolk County Department of Health Service's Office of Ecology and the Service developed an agreement to perform an inventory of SAV and hardened shorelines in 2000. Work on this project was initiated upon receipt of the aerial photos. This report presents the results of this inventory. Maps showing the distribution of submerged aquatic vegetation beds, hardened shorelines, and docks are located in the Appendices (Appendix A for distribution of SAV beds and Appendix B for hardened shorelines and docks).

Study Area

The study area is the Peconic Bay Estuary on the eastern end of Long Island, New York (Figure 1). It includes parts of 12-1:24,000 maps on the eastern end of Long Island: Montauk Point, Gardiners Island East, Gardiners Island West, Plum Island, Orient, Greenport, Southold, Napeague Beach, Sag Harbor, Southampton, Mattituck, and Riverhead. Five towns are located in the study area: East Hampton, Riverhead, Shelter Island, Southampton, and Southold.

Figure 1. Location of Peconic Estuary in eastern Long Island, New York. The map at the bottom of the page shows towns and the limits of 1:24,000 maps (rectangles not labeled).

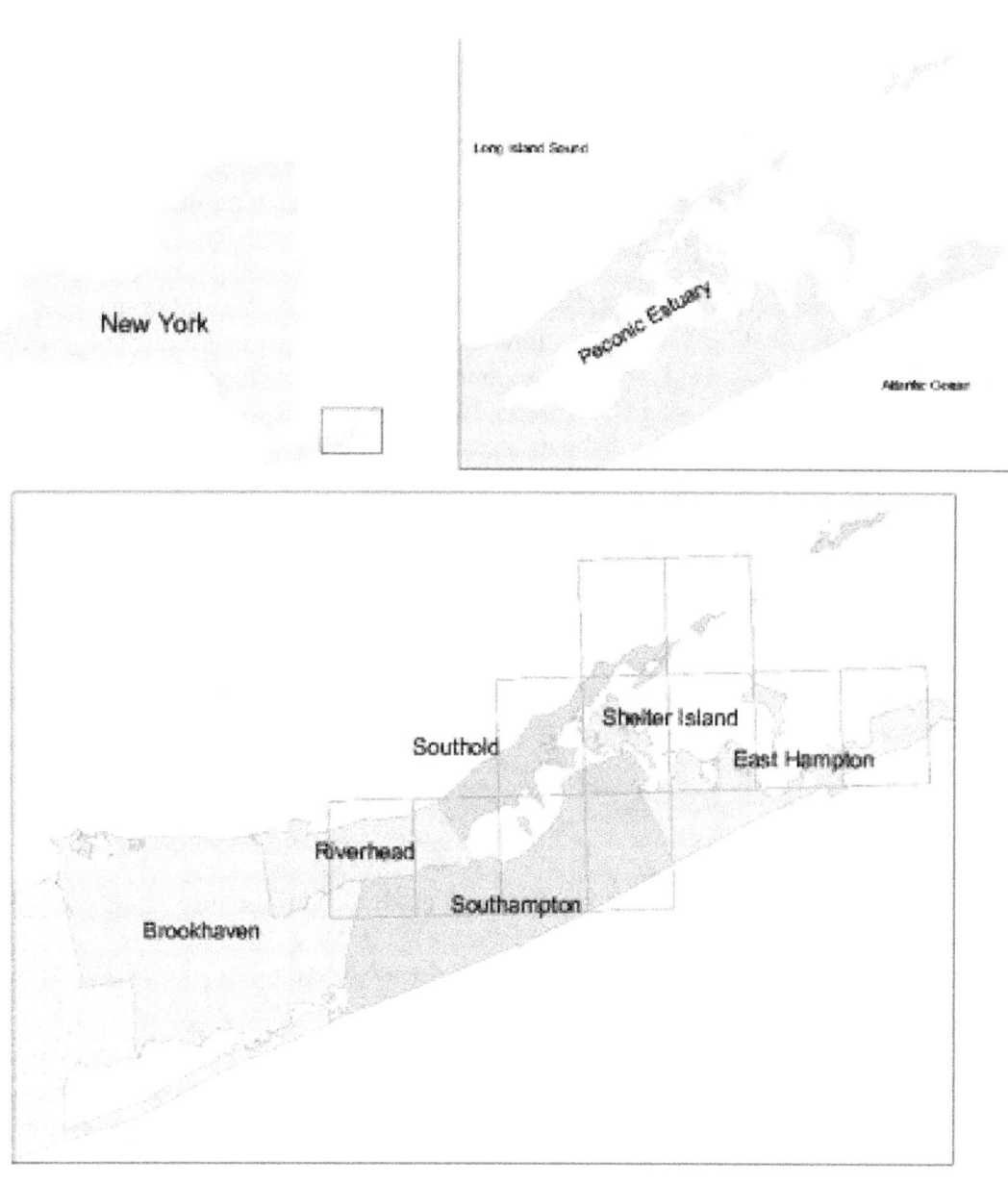

Methods

Conventional aerial photointerpretation techniques were used to identify SAV beds and hardened shorelines. A digital transfer scope (DTS) was used to delineate these features onto digital orthophotoquarterquads (DOQQs). The DOQQs represented the most accurate representation of current shoreline features for geopositioning hardened shoreline features and SAV beds. Aerial photographs used for this project were 1:14,400 true color photos acquired from September to November 2000 by PEP. The scale, emulsion, and environmental conditions generally complied with the National Oceanic and Atmospheric Administration's Coastal Change Analysis Program (C-CAP) protocols for mapping SAV beds (Dobson et al. 1995; posted on the internet at: http://www.csc.noaa.gov/products/maine/html/sav2.htm), except that photography was flown in the fall instead of June. June is best for detection of eelgrass (Zostera marina). Although the photography was clear and in general provided good depth resolution, the timing of this photography was not ideal for separating eelgrass from other aquatic species. Many other species (especially algae) were present in the water at this time. SAV beds were classified into four cover classes based on relative densities: 100%, 75%, 50%, and 25%. Extensive field work was required to characterize the vegetation in most beds.

Seven categories of hardened shorelines were also inventoried (Table 1); docks were mapped as well. Photointerpreters identified these categories through conventional aerial photointerpretation techniques. The quality of the photos and season allowed for accurate detection of these features. While most shoreline features were mapped as linear features (i.e., line segments), some structures (e.g., permanent piers, breakwaters, and jetties) were large enough to map as polygons. Since the reason for mapping the latter features was to determine the extent of hardened shorelines, the waterward perimeter of these structures were measured as linear features. Hardened shoreline data are reported in linear dimensions (i.e., linear miles for the entire estuary and linear feet for towns and critical natural resource areas).

Draft maps were prepared and sent to PEP and Cornell Cooperative Extension Marine Program for review. Ground truthing of SAV beds and of hardened shorelines was performed by Chris Pickerell and Steve Schott (Cornell Cooperative Extension) and Kevin McAllister (Peconic BayKeeper), respectively. Review comments were received in 2002 for most areas and in mid-2003 for Gardiners Island and the data were updated accordingly. Several types of SAV beds were identified by field reviewers: algae, red algae (Rhodophyta), eelgrass, green fleece or dead man's fingers (Codium fragile), rockweed (Fucus/Ascophyllum), sea lettuce (Ulva lactuca), widgeon-grass (Ruppia maritima), and various mixtures of these types. Unmapped beds observed in the field were added to the database based on field sketches and subsequent photointerpretation. Where possible, they were placed in the applicable SAV cover class. Some field-identified beds were not visible on the aerial photos and could not be classified to cover class. Two sets of eleven quad-based (1:24,000) maps were prepared: one set showing location, shape, and type of SAV and the other set showing hardened shoreline extent and types. (Note: The Gardiners Island East map includes part of the Napeague Beach quadrangle since only a small portion of this quadrangle occurred in the Peconic Estuary.)

For the report, data were summarized for the entire estuary, by town, and by critical natural resource (CNR) area. Sixteen CNR areas are located in the study area: Arshamonaque, Cedar Beach, Cow Neck, Cutchogue, Flanders Bay, Gardiners Island, Jessups Neck, Long Island Pine Barrens, Montauk, Northwest Harbor, Orient, Plum Island, Richmond Creek/Jockey Creek, Robins Island, Shelter Island, and Threemile/Accobonac Harbor (Figure 2). For GIS analysis and map production, the boundaries of these features came from digital data provided by PEP.

Table 1. Hardened shoreline types for the Peconic Estuary inventory project.

Feature (map code)	Definition
Breakwater (BW)	exposed or submerged rock structure that is usually constructed to protect a shore, harbor, or basin from wave action; often built more or less parallel to the shoreline
Bulkhead and Seawall (BK)	wood, steel, or concrete structure or stone rubble to provide limited protection of shoreline from wave action
Groin (GR)	rock, steel, timber, or concrete structure constructed more or less perpendicular to the beach for the purpose of trapping sand for the beach
Jetty (JT)	dumped stone or rubble mound constructed at the mouth of an inlet to stabilize the opening and prevent inlet migration
Permanent Pier (PP)*	solid stone or concrete pier (not suspended on piling) that restricts water circulation
Other Significant Pier (OSP)	large piers or wharves on solid fill or piling
Revetment (RR)	rock or concrete riprap placed along the shore to form a gentle sloping feature for stabilizing shoreline and reducing wave-caused shoreline erosion
Dock (DK)**	wooden structure built on pilings and typically consisting of a boardwalk and floating platform for mooring a boat

*Mapped as polygons with linear dimensions calculated and entered as bulkhead/seawall.

**Not actually a hardened shoreline, but included in the analysis per request from the Peconic Estuary Program.

Figure 2. Location of critical natural resource areas associated with the Peconic Estuary.

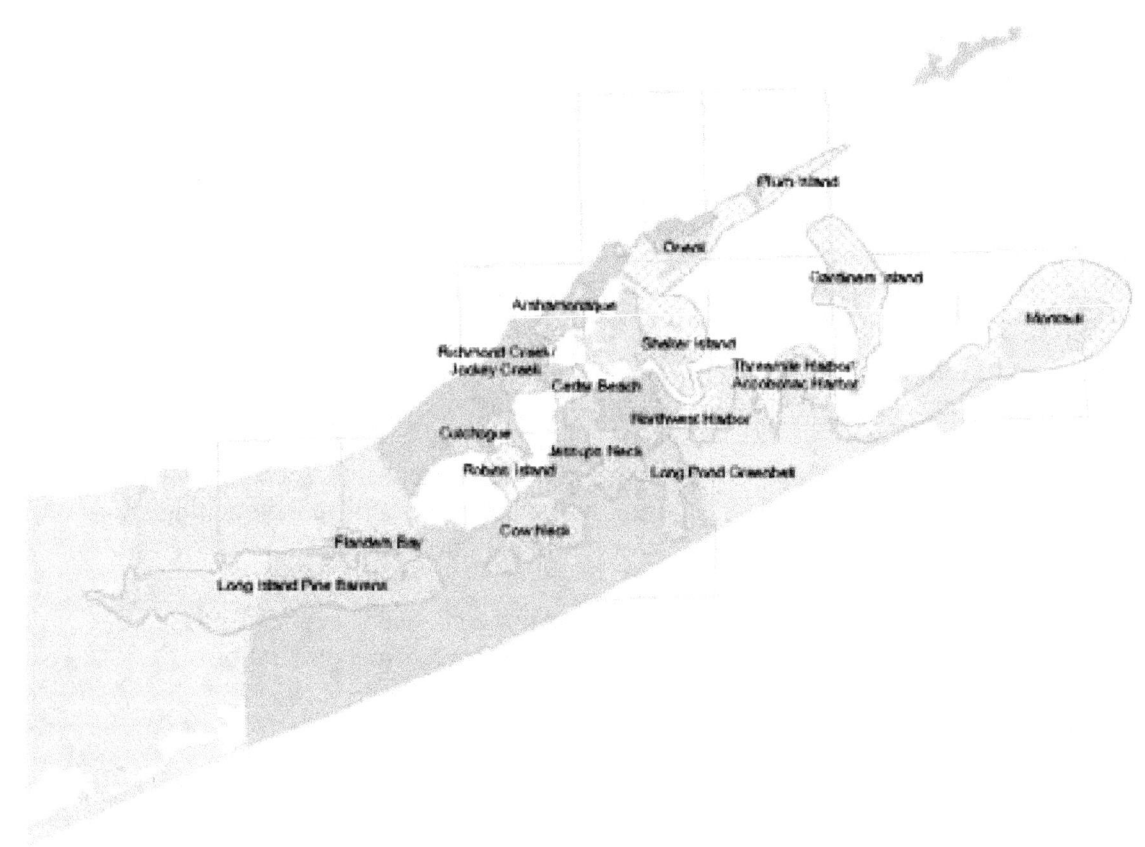

Results

Submerged Aquatic Vegetation

A total of 1,339 beds comprising 3,539 acres of submerged aquatic vegetation (SAV) was inventoried in the Peconic Estuary (Table 2). Eelgrass (Figure 3) and "other algae" occupied over 2,660 acres, accounting for about three-quarters of the bed acreage (44% and 31%, respectively). Green fleece (including mixtures with red algae) accounted for about 11 percent of the SAV acreage.

East Hampton had the most acreage of SAV beds of the townships falling within the Peconic Estuary (Table 3). It alone possessed 36 percent of the Estuary's SAV beds. Eelgrass was nearly even distributed among three towns (East Hampton - 33%; Shelter Island - 32%, and Southold - 28%).

Of the critical natural resource (CNR) areas, Gardiners Island (687 acres), Shelter Island (599), and Orient (410) were top-ranked in SAV abundance (Table 4).

The distribution of SAV beds is shown on a series of maps (Appendix A).

Figure 3. View of eelgrass bed taken by underwater camera.

Table 2. Extent of submerged aquatic vegetation (SAV) in the Peconic Estuary.
<u>Note</u>: Unknown cover is based on field surveys where beds were not photointerpretable
on the imagery used for this inventory and no cover estimates were made.

SAV Type	100% Cover acres (# of beds)	75% Cover acres (#)	50% Cover acres (#)	25% Cover acres (#)	Unknown Cover acres (#)	Total acres (#)
Other Algae	442.1 (182)	490.7 (105)	109.1 (42)	70.2 (28)	0 -	1,112.1 (357)
Green Fleece	26.8 (6)	56.4 (14)	66.2 (11)	29.1 (2)	12.9 (2)	191.4 (35)
Green Fleece/ Red Algae	147.8 (325)	35.3 (25)	16.4 (28)	7.1 (15)	0 -	206.6 (393)
Eelgrass	459.9 (21)	705.9 (54)	362.3 (34)	20.9 (8)	1.2 (2)	1,550.2 (119)
Eelgrass/ Algae	0 -	0 -	1.8 (1)	0 -	0 -	1.8 (1)
Rockweed	0 -	0 -	0 -	0.8 (1)	0 -	0.8 (1)
Widgeon-grass	0 -	8.9 (5)	0 -	5.4 (1)	0 -	14.3 (6)
Widgeon-grass/Algae	9.8 (3)	0 -	5.6 (3)	0 -	0 -	15.4 (6)
Sea Lettuce	10.8 (7)	10.3 (5)	7.1 (2)	0 -	0 -	28.2 (14)
Unknown	78.7 (201)	198.2 (116)	99.0 (50)	42.3 (40)	0 -	418.2 (407)
Total						*3,539.0 (1,339)*

Table 3. Extent of SAV beds by township for the Peconic Estuary. Unknown SAV type represents beds that were not field checked. Note that the number of beds is greater than the total listed for the Estuary proper as individual beds were separated by town lines.

Town	SAV Type	Acreage by Cover Class (# of beds)					Total Acres (# of beds)
		100%	75%	50%	25%	Unknown	
East Hampton	Other Algae	191.4 (4)	307.5 (79)	17.0 (12)	4.3 (1)	0	520.2 (96)
	Green Fleece	0 -	18.2 (1)	50.3 (6)	0 -	12.9 (3)	81.4 (10)
	Eelgrass	331.8 (7)	98.4 (38)	63.0 (15)	18.6 (4)	0.2 (3)	512.0 (67)
	Widgeon-grass	0 -	4.5 (9)	0 -	0 -	0 -	4.5 (9)
	Unknown	5.5 (9)	68.1 (49)	71.8 (24)	6.7 (4)	0 -	152.1 (86)
	Total						1,270.2 (268)
Riverhead	Other Algae	4.7 (9)	0 -	0 -	0 -	0 -	4.7 (9)
	Green Fleece	56.1 (101)	2.0 (1)	2.4 (1)	1.6 (2)	0 -	62.1 (105)
	Unknown	3.6 (16)	0.2 (1)	<0.1 (1)	0 -	0 -	3.8 (18)
	Total						70.6 (132)
Shelter Island	Other Algae	3.3 (8)	36.6 (44)	10.8 (9)	0.4 (2)	0 -	51.1 (63)
	Green Fleece	5.7 (2)	26.2 (16)	8.8 (8)	0 -	0 -	40.7 (26)
	Eelgrass	7.0 (7)	365.2 (24)	114.2 (15)	2.3 (5)	0 -	488.7 (51)
	Unknown	15.7 (12)	77.2 (58)	10.0 (13)	11.3 (5)	0 -	114.2 (88)
	Total						694.7 (228)

9

Table 3 (cont'd).

Town	SAV Type	Acreage by Cover Class (# of beds)					Total Acres (# of beds)
		100%	75%	50%	25%	Unknown	
Southampton	Other Algae	211.5 (143)	43.2 (12)	40.6 (18)	41.8 (18)	0 -	337.1 (191)
	Green Fleece	21.1 (4)	0.4 (1)	3.0 (2)	1.4 (1)	0	25.9 (8)
	Green Fleece w/Red Algae	91.7 (224)	33.3 (24)	14.0 (27)	5.5 (13)	0	144.5 (288)
	Eelgrass	117.7 (16)	7.4 (4)	0 -	0 -	0 -	125.1 (20)
	Widgeon-grass	8.1 (1)	0 -	0 -	0 -	0 -	8.1 (1)
	Unknown	36.2 (77)	28.6 (15)	11.0 (13)	11.8 (19)	0 -	87.6 (124)
	Total						*728.3 (632)*
Southold	Other Algae	31.1 (45)	103.4 (69)	40.7 (25)	24.5 (24)	0 -	199.7 (163)
	Green Fleece	0 -	11.6 (6)	4.1 (1)	27.6 (2)	0 -	43.3 (9)
	Eelgrass	3.6 (1)	234.9 (26)	185.1 (36)	0 -	1.0 (1)	424.6 (64)
	Eelgrass w/Algae	0 -	0 -	1.8 (2)	0 -	0 -	1.8 (2)
	Sea Lettuce	10.8 (7)	10.3 (9)	7.1 (2)	0 -	0 -	28.2 (18)
	Widgeon-grass	1.7* (5)	4.4 (5)	5.6* (4)	5.4 (1)	0 -	17.1 (15)
	Unknown	17.8 (109)	24.1 (32)	6.1 (13)	12.5 (18)	0 -	60.5 (172)
	Total						*775.2 (443)*

*mixed with/algae

Table 4. Extent of SAV beds within CNR areas for the Peconic Estuary. <u>Note</u>: Algae includes sea lettuce.

CNR Area	SAV Type	No. of Beds	Acres
Arshamonaque	Other Algae	7	12.8
	Eelgrass	9	34.8
	Unknown	6	2.4
	Total	*22*	*50.0*
Cedar Beach	Eelgrass	1	1.0
	Widgeon-grass/Algae	2	3.6
	Unknown	1	0.2
	Total	*4*	*4.8*
Cow Neck	Other Algae	149	246.1
	Eelgrass	5	83.7
	Total	*154*	*329.8*
Cutchogue	Other Algae	45	56.0
	Green Fleece	1	6.0
	Widgeon-grass	2	9.2
	Unknown	40	13.0
	Total	*88*	*84.2*
Flanders Bay	Other Algae	14	57.4
	Green Fleece/Red Algae	379	176.3
	Unknown	19	10.4
	Total	*412*	*244.1*
Gardiners Island	Other Algae	18	417.9
	Eelgrass	2	233.3
	Unknown	12	35.7
	Total	*31*	*686.9*
Jessups Neck	Other Algae	16	2.4
	Green Fleece	7	18.8
	Eelgrass	8	2.3
	Unknown	33	3.4
	Total	*64*	*26.9*
Long Island Pine Barrens	Green Fleece	3	0.1
	Unknown	1	0.2
	Total	*4*	*0.3*
Long Pond Greenbelt	*Algae (=Total)*	*1*	*1.4*

Table 4 (cont'd)

CNR Area	SAV Type	No. of Beds	Acres
Montauk	Other Algae	13	44.0
	Green Fleece	3	33.0
	Eelgrass	12	140.7
	Unknown	6	6.2
	Total	*34*	*223.9*
Northwest Harbor	Other Algae	11	19.8
	Green Fleece	1	6.7
	Eelgrass	21	104.8
	Unknown	72	121.5
	Total	*105*	*252.8*
Orient	Other Algae	12	24.6
	Green Fleece	4	37.4
	Eelgrass	20	333.6
	Widgeon-grass	3	0.6
	Unknown	6	13.9
	Total	*45*	*410.1*
Richmond Creek/ Jockey Creek	Other Algae	10	17.3
	Widgeon-grass	3	3.7
	Unknown	29	15.7
	Total	*42*	*36.7*
Robins Island	Algae	14	77.7
Shelter Island	Other Algae	8	21.3
	Green Fleece	10	33.3
	Eelgrass	20	476.3
	Unknown	25	68.1
	Total	*63*	*599.0*
Threemile Harbor/ Accobonac Harbor	Other Algae	17	47.3
	Green Fleece	5	48.4
	Eelgrass	18	61.1
	Widgeon-grass	1	4.5
	Unknown	19	36.5
	Total	*60*	*197.8*

Hardened Shorelines and Docks

Hardened shorelines and docks were inventoried for the Peconic Estuary (see Figure 4 for examples). All data are reported in linear miles or feet. Almost 29 miles of hardened shorelines and nearly 9 miles of docks were mapped (Table 5). Eighty-two percent of the hardened shorelines were comprised of bulkheads and seawalls.

Of the five towns in the Estuary, Southold had the greatest length of hardened shorelines overall (more than 66,000 feet or 12.6 miles) and in all individual categories, except breakwaters (Table 6). It possessed almost twice the length of bulkheads and seawalls as Southampton, the second-ranked town. Southold also had the most docks (625) and the longest total dock length (2.8 miles). Shelter Island and Southampton had nearly equal total dock length, with the latter having slightly more docks (405 v. 367).

Of the CNR areas, Northwest Harbor and Arshamonaque had more than 2.0 miles of hardened shorelines (Table 7). Other areas with more than one mile of hardened shorelines were Cow Neck, Cutchogue, Shelter Island, and Threemile/Accobonac Harbors. Northwest Harbor had greatest length of docks, with nearly one mile (5,380.5 feet) of these structures. Montauk and Cutchogue had more than 4,000 feet of docks.

The distribution of hardened shorelines and docks is shown on a series of maps in Appendix B.

Figure 4. Examples of hardened shoreline features (a-c) and dock (d).
(photos by The Nature Conservancy)

Table 5. Extent of hardened shorelines and docks in the Peconic Estuary. (<u>Note</u>: Bulkhead/seawall data include those associated with permanent piers.)

Feature	Length in Miles (number)
Bulkhead/Seawall	23.6 (653)*
Breakwater	1.1 (23)
Dock	8.7 (1,636)
Groin	1.5 (412)
Jetty	0.9 (11)
Other Significant Pier	0.8 (42)
Revetment	0.7 (23)
Total	37.3 (2,800)
Total minus Dock Length	28.6 (1,164)

*Includes bulkheads surrounding 62 permanent piers (68.9 acres).

Table 6. Extent of hardened shorelines and docks for towns in the Peconic Estuary. Grand totals may differ slightly from totals for Estuary since a single structure could occur in more than one town. (Note: Bulkhead/seawall data include those associated with permanent piers.)

Town	Hardened Shore Feature	Feet of Hardened Shore (number)	Feet of Docks (number)
East Hampton	Bulkhead/Seawall	16,278.5 (87)	5,839.7 (122)
	Breakwater	2,215.7 (11)	
	Groin	1,312.2 (49)	
	Jetty	631.4 (2)	
	Other Significant Pier	1,416.4 (19)	
	Revetment	1,030.2 (5)	
	Total	*22,884,4 (173)*	
Riverhead	Bulkhead/Seawall	12,655.6 (73)	3,584.3 (142)
	Groin	737.5 (37)	
	Other Significant Pier	121.9 (1)	
	Revetment	136.4 (2)	
	Total	*13,651.4 (113)*	
Shelter Island	Bulkhead/Seawall	17,263.0 (88)	10,869.5 (367)
	Groin	1,680.6 (85)	
	Other Significant Pier	184.9 (3)	
	Total	*19,129.5 (176)*	
Southampton	Bulkhead/Seawall	23,440.3 (164)	10,763.1 (405)
	Breakwater	1,510.0 (2)	
	Groin	476.7 (26)	
	Jetty	1,759.1 (2)	
	Other Significant Pier	744.9 (8)	
	Revetment	837.3 (7)	
	Total	*28,768.3 (209)*	
Southold	Bulkhead/Seawall	55,109.9 (335)	14,953.0 (625)
	Breakwater	1,903.8 (18)	
	Groin	3,800.5 (215)	
	Jetty	2,124.6 (10)	
	Other Significant Pier	1,779.2 (14)	
	Revetment	1,807.4 (11)	
	Total	*66,525.4 (603)*	

Table 7. Extent of hardened shorelines and docks for CNR areas in the Peconic Estuary. (Note: Bulkhead/seawall data include those associated with permanent piers.)

CNR Area	Hardened Shore Feature	Feet of Hardened Shore (number)	Feet of Docks (number)
Arshamonaque	Bulkhead/Seawall	8,267.9 (33)	1,973.3 (43)
	Breakwater	602.1 (5)	
	Groin	408.0 (16)	
	Jetty	830.8 (2)	
	Revetment	385.6 (3)	
	Total	*10,494.4 (59)*	
Cedar Beach	Bulkhead/Seawall	2,627.2 (16)	697.5 (37)
	Groin	464.0 (25)	
	Total	*3,091.2 (41)*	
Cow Neck	Bulkhead/Seawall	5,755.3 (56)	2,632.1 (119)
	Revetment	443.5 (5)	
	Total	*6,198.8 (61)*	
Cutchogue	Bulkhead/Seawall	6,287.6 (73)	4,408.1 (206)
	Breakwater	716.6 (3)	
	Groin	763.6 (43)	
	Revetment	308.2 (3)	
	Total	*8,076.0 (122)*	
Flanders Bay	Bulkhead/Seawall	2,846.0 (24)	2,157.3 (78)
	Groin	52.7 (2)	
	Other Significant Pier	121.9 (1)	
	Revetment	261.1 (3)	
	Total	*3,281.7 (30)*	
Gardiners Island	Bulkhead/Seawall	154.1 (2)	-
	Breakwater	84.0 (1)	
	Groin	15.8 (1)	
	Revetment	31.5 (1)	
	Total	*285.4 (5)*	
Jessups Neck	Bulkhead/Seawall	1,254.2 (10)	923.8 (46)
	Other Significant Pier	181.9 (2)	
	Total	*1,436.1 (12)*	
Long Island Pine Barrens	Bulkhead/Seawall	2,196.3 (14)	63.4 (5)
	Groin	48.7 (8)	
	Total	*2,245.0 (22)*	

Table 7 (cont'd).

Montauk	Bulkhead/Seawall	1,936.7 (8)	4,105.6 (65)
	Groin	323.3 (11)	
	Jetty	631.4 (2)	
	Other Significant Pier	306.1 (2)	
	Revetment	41.3 (1)	
	Total	*3,238.8 (24)*	
Northwest Harbor	Bulkhead/Seawall	8,421.7 (47)	5,380.5 (198)
	Breakwater	3,358.5 (4)	
	Groin	261.3 (11)	
	Other Significant Pier	563.0 (6)	
	Total	*12,604.5 (68)*	
Orient	Bulkhead/Seawall	1,640.4 (14)	813.0 (25)
	Groin	410.4 (27)	
	Jetty	9.8 (1)	
	Revetment	901.7 (3)	
	Total	*2,962.3 (45)*	
Plum Island	Groin	38.3 (1)	-
	Total	*38.3 (1)*	
Richmond/Jockey Creeks	Bulkhead/Seawall	4,599.2 (39)	2,181.0 (121)
	Breakwater	66.5 (1)	
	Groin	82.5 (4)	
	Jetty	200.7 (2)	
	Total	*4,949.2 (46)*	
Robins Island	Other Significant Pier	91.0 (2)	
	Total	*91.0 (2)*	
Shelter Island	Bulkhead/Seawall	4,703.2 (30)	2,300.3 (75)
	Groin	900.2 (45)	
	Other Significant Pier	112.9 (3)	
	Total	*5,716.3 (78)*	
Threemile/Accobonac Harbors	Bulkhead/Seawall	5,495.5 (31)	367.0 (22)
	Breakwater	283.2 (4)	
	Groin	483.2 (21)	
	Other Significant Pier	1,079.1 (17)	
	Revetment	857.0 (2)	
	Total	*8,198.0 (75)*	

Conclusions

The purpose of this study was to record the current status (Year 2000) of submerged aquatic vegetation, hardened shorelines, and docks in the Peconic Estuary. During this survey, we developed more insight into this type of work and offer the following remarks.

1. Aerial Photography. The aerial photography provided for this project was acquired in the fall of 2000. Although water clarity was generally excellent, there was a great deal of macroalgae present. Substantial field work was required to separate algal beds from rooted vascular aquatics and to verify species composition. If interested primarily in mapping eelgrass and other rooted vascular aquatic species, it is best to capture photographs during the time of peak productivity. The National Oceanic and Atmospheric Administration's Coastal Change Analysis Program offers guidelines for monitoring submerged land using aerial photography (Dobson et al. 1995). According to this source, June is the best time to acquire photography for mapping submersed rooted vascular plants in the Northeast. The Cornell Cooperative Extension has been conducting site-specific studies of eelgrass and should be able to determine the optimal time for eelgrass detection (i.e., maximum standing crop/biomass). The photography used for the current survey maximized detection of aquatic species, but may have not been the best for eelgrass detection. By fall, some eelgrass beds may have die-backed, while others may have become smaller in size. Eelgrass mapping projects in Rhode Island and Long Island Sound have used June photography (e.g., Tiner et al. 2003). While June may be best for SAV bed detection, is it the best time for identifying seasonal docks? PEP will need to consider this if such photography is designed to serve a multi-purpose (i.e., monitoring SAV, hardened shorelines, and docks) for future projects.

2. Need for SAV Monitoring Studies. The current inventory represents a single snapshot of the status of eelgrass and other submerged aquatic beds in the Peconic Estuary. We have no information on the stability or dynamics of these beds. Are the results of this survey valid for the current decade or do they represent a peak or trough in the natural dynamics of SAV growth? To determine what are typical or "normal" conditions, periodic surveys are necessary. SAV mapping in the Chesapeake Bay has been conducted on an annual basis for many years to document fluctuations in these beds due to their importance to the Bay's living aquatic resources. This cyclical information is especially important for coastal resource management as such studies are necessary to document recovery due to reduced pollution inputs or to other management strategies employed to promote SAV growth and improve water quality. Annual SAV studies are recommended to obtain a better understanding of the natural dynamics or stability of the beds in the Peconic Estuary. The costs of such studies should be less than the current work as a geospatial database has been created and can form the foundation for future assessments.

3. Monitoring Trends in Shoreline Development. This survey identifies the extent of hardened shoreline and dock construction in the Estuary in the Year 2000. Given the

impact of this type of development on coastal resources and the rise in sea level, it would be worthwhile to conduct periodic assessments of these features. Such work could be coupled with the SAV monitoring studies referenced above, so annual surveys could be conducted. Given the creation of a geospatial database with the 2000 status recorded and the permanence of most of the structures, the costs of monitoring these trends should be considerably less than the original cost. If annual monitoring is not feasible, then monitoring at 5-year intervals should be performed, at a minimum.

4. <u>Targeting Wetlands Vulnerable to Sea Level Rise</u>. The results of this study when coupled with other information (e.g., National Wetlands Inventory data and SAV inventory data) can be used to identify areas that may be particular vulnerable to change due to sea level rise. It is a recognized fact that as sea level rises, coastal wetlands move landward. If hardened shorelines or other barriers are constructed on the landward side of tidal wetlands or aquatic beds, these habitats will be squeezed out of existence. Coastal planners need to develop strategies to permit natural transgression processes to occur. Sufficient open land (undeveloped; not commercial, industrial, or residential land) must be preserved landward of the marshes to allow for natural migration of tidal marshes resulting from rising sea level.

Acknowledgments

This inventory was undertaken at the request of and with support from the Peconic Estuary Program of the Suffolk County Department of Health Services, Office of Ecology. Walter Dawydiak served as project officer for this effort, with assistance from Laura Bavaro. The Cornell Cooperative Extension, Marine Program (CMP) was actively involved in this project. Steve Schott was the point person for CMP and was instrumental in overseeing field review of draft maps. Ralph Tiner directed the project for the U.S. Fish and Wildlife Service (FWS), and was responsible for project design, data analysis, and report preparation.

Photointerpretation and digital database construction were accomplished by Denise Siraco (University of Massachusetts) and Herbert Bergquist (FWS), with John Swords (FWS) providing quality control. Bobbi Jo McClain (FWS) performed GIS processing, data compilation, and map production. Mr. Bergquist revised selected maps and statistics based on input from the PEP in mid-2003.

Kevin McAllister, Peconic BayKeeper, conducted field review of hardened shoreline features which was coordinated by Chris Smith (CMP). Field inspections of SAV beds were performed by Steve Schott, Chris Pickerell, and Lorne Brousseau (CMP) and by the following representatives of the East Hampton Town Natural Resources Department: Kristin Knobloch, Bob Masin, Andrew Gates, Megan Shaffer, Jessica Hok, Bill Taylor, Ian Bach, Walter Galcik, and Larry Penny. Their efforts are greatly appreciated as the inventory would not have been as detailed and comprehensive without their contributions.

Wayne Grothe of The Nature Conservancy kindly provided photos of shoreline features for use as Figure 4 in this report.

References

Dobson, J.E., E.A. Bright, R.L. Ferguson, D.W. Field, L.L. Wood, K.D. Haddad, H. Iredale III, J.R. Jensen, V.V. Klemas, R.J. Orth, and J.P. Thomas. 1995. NOAA Coastal Change Analysis Program (C-CAP): Guidance for Regional Implementation. U.S. Department of Commerce, Seattle, WA. NOAA Technical Report NMFS 123.

Tiner, R., H. Bergquist, T. Halavick, and A. MacLachlan. 2003. Eelgrass Survey for Eastern Long Island Sound, Connecticut and New York. U.S. Fish and Wildlife Service, National Wetlands Inventory (NWI) Program, Northeast Region, Hadley, MA. NWI technical report.

Appendices

Appendix A.

Maps showing the distribution of SAV beds in the Peconic Estuary

(<u>Note</u>: The Gardiners Island East map includes part of the Napeague Beach quadrangle)

Peconic Estuary Submerged Aquatic Vegetation
Gardiners Island East Quadrangle

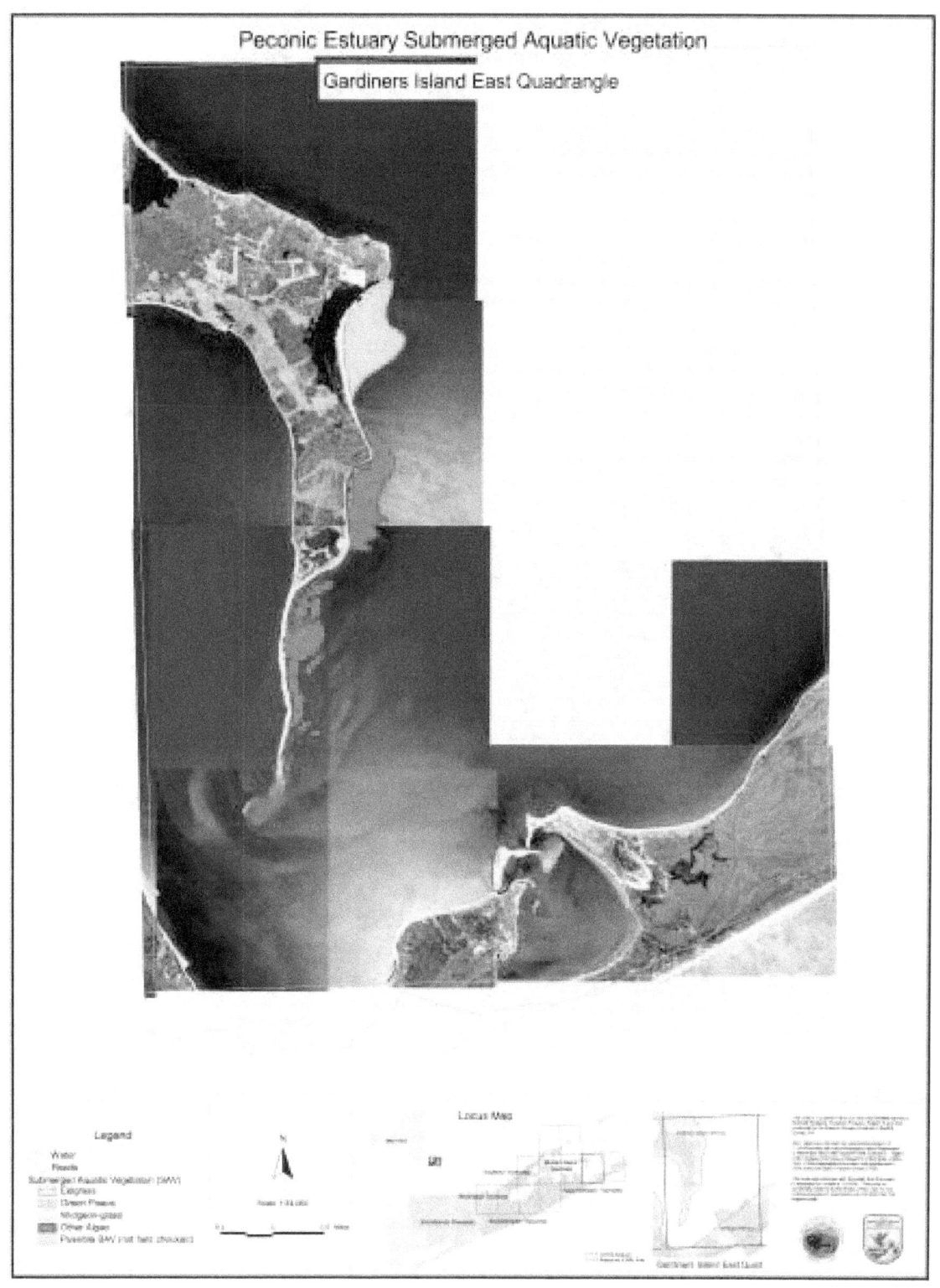

Peconic Estuary Submerged Aquatic Vegetation
Gardiners Island West Quadrangle

Legend

Water
Roads
Submerged Aquatic Vegetation (SAV)
Eelgrass
Green Fleece
Widgeon-grass
Other Algae
Possible SAV (not field checked)

Locus Map

Peconic Estuary Submerged Aquatic Vegetation
Greenport Quadrangle

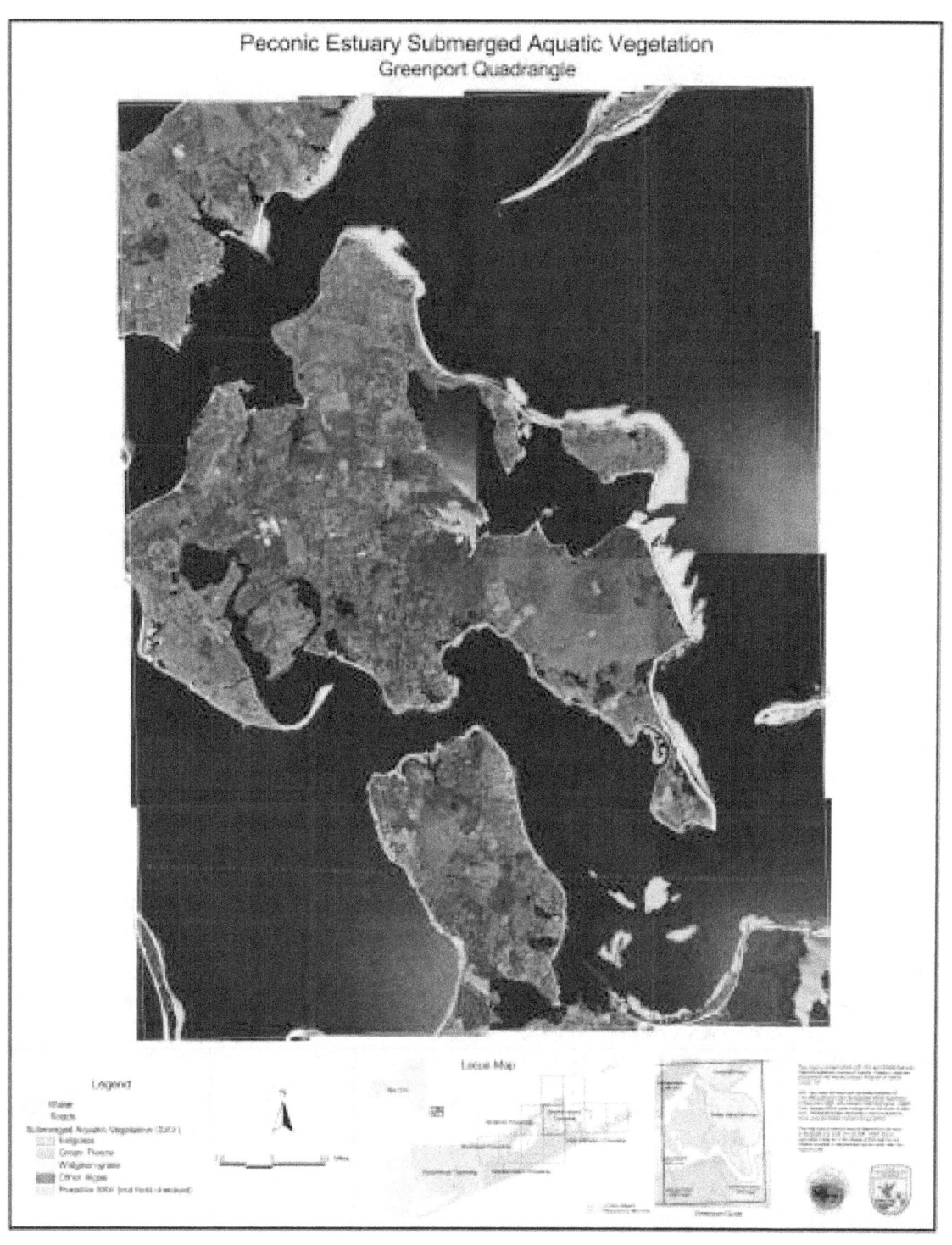

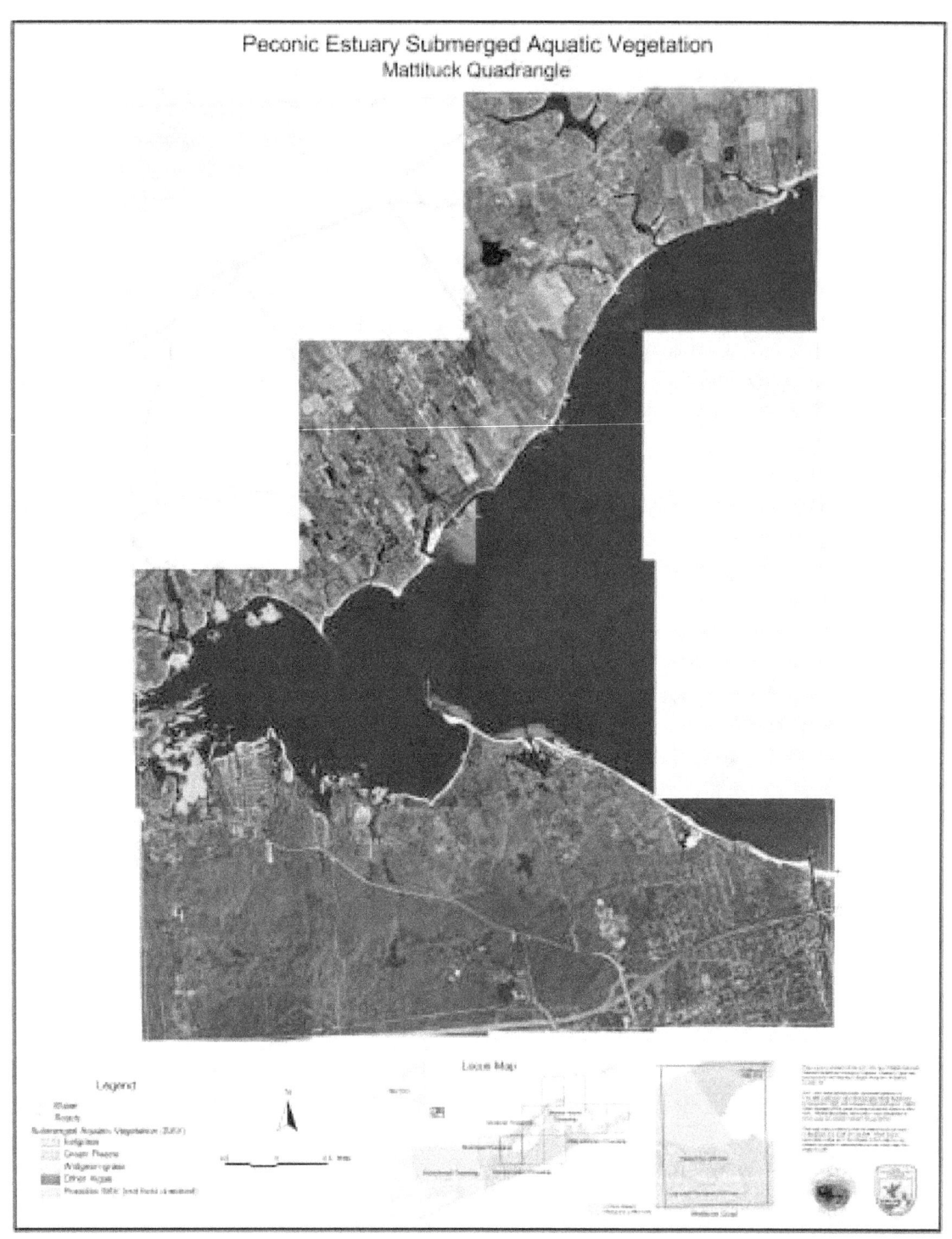

Peconic Estuary Submerged Aquatic Vegetation
Mattituck Quadrangle

28

Peconic Estuary Submerged Aquatic Vegetation
Montauk Point Quadrangle

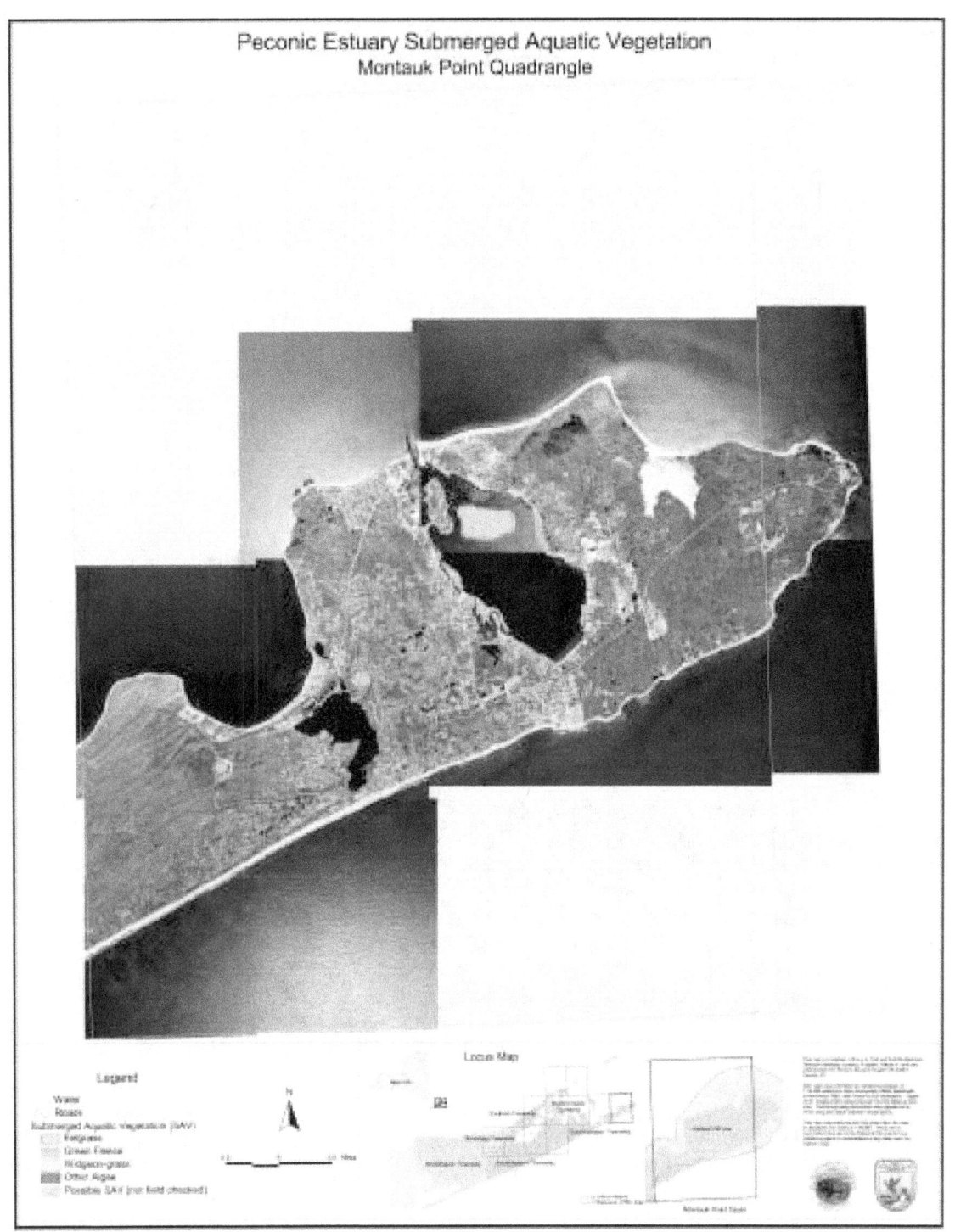

Peconic Estuary Submerged Aquatic Vegetation
Orient Quadrangle

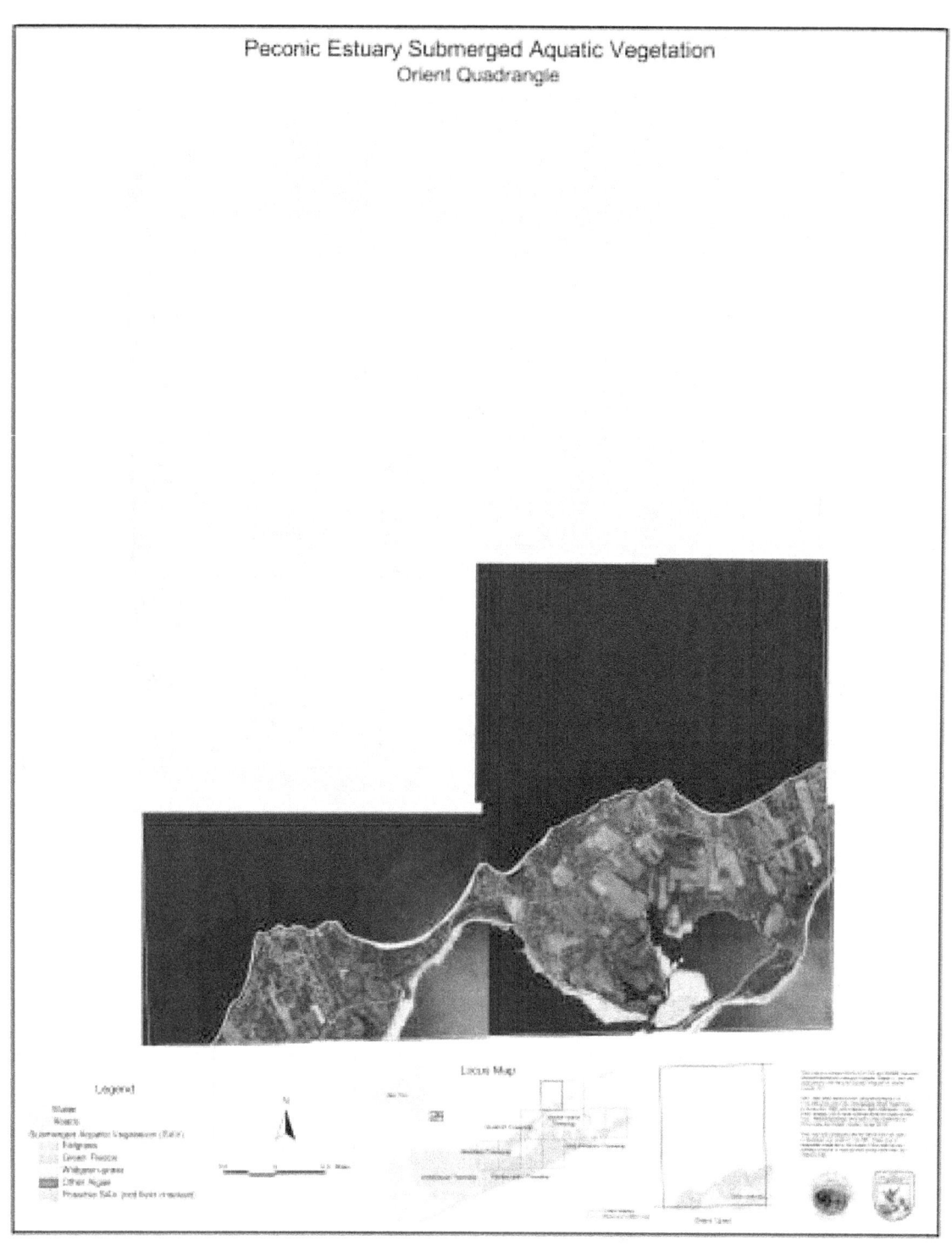

Peconic Estuary Submerged Aquatic Vegetation
Plum Island Quadrangle

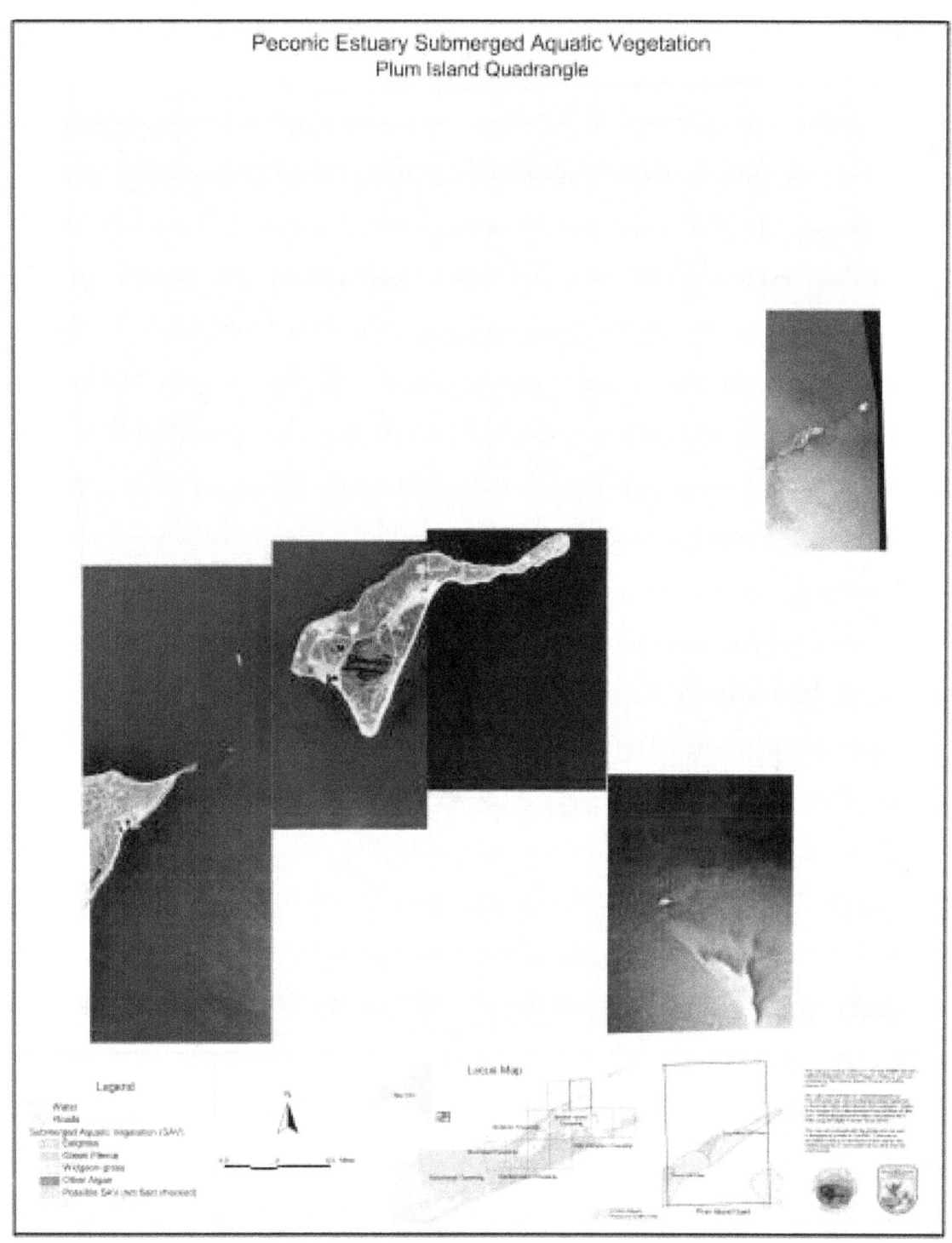

Peconic Estuary Submerged Aquatic Vegetation
Riverhead Quadrangle

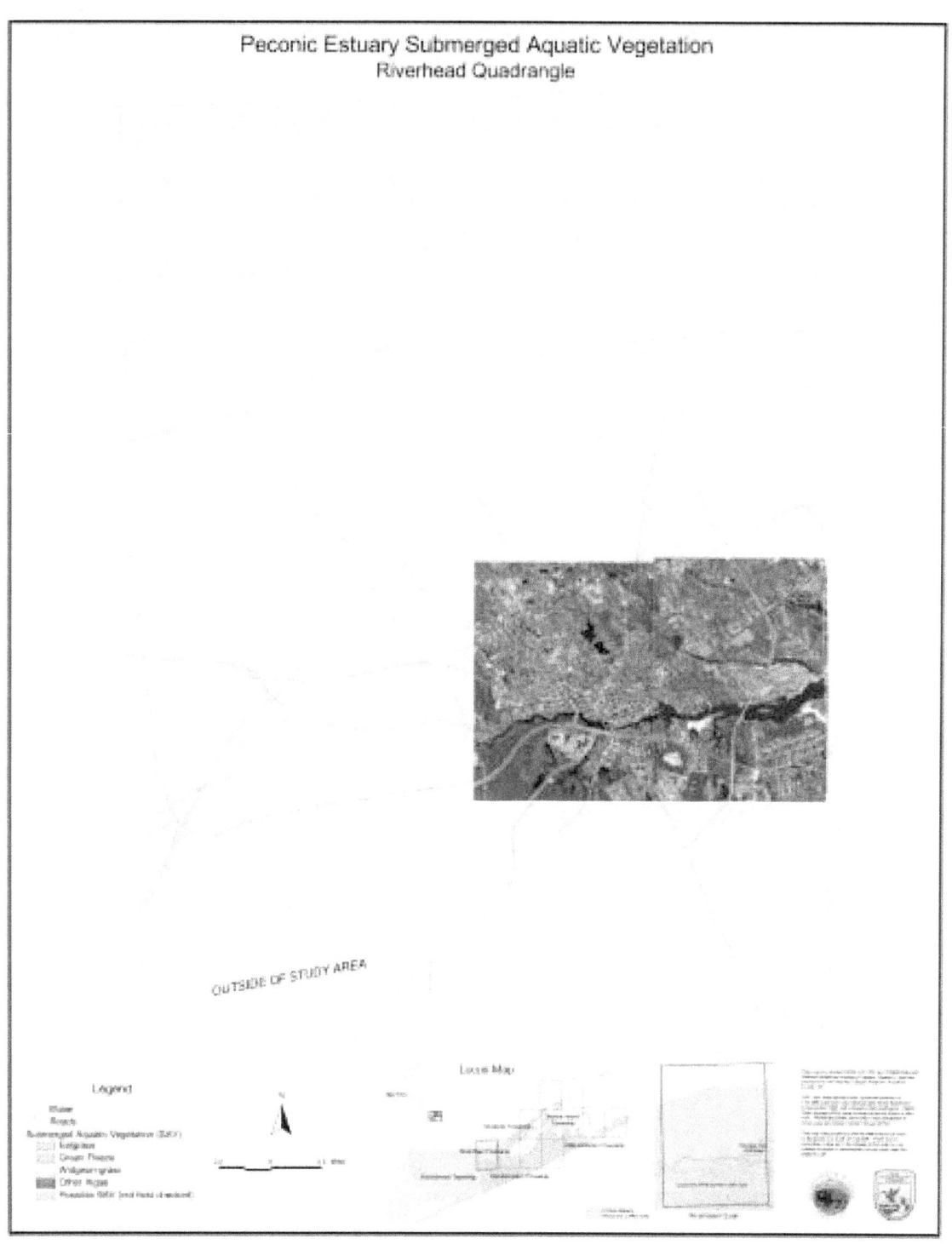

OUTSIDE OF STUDY AREA

Peconic Estuary Submerged Aquatic Vegetation
Sag Harbor Quadrangle

OUTSIDE OF STUDY AREA

Peconic Estuary Submerged Aquatic Vegetation
Southampton Quadrangle

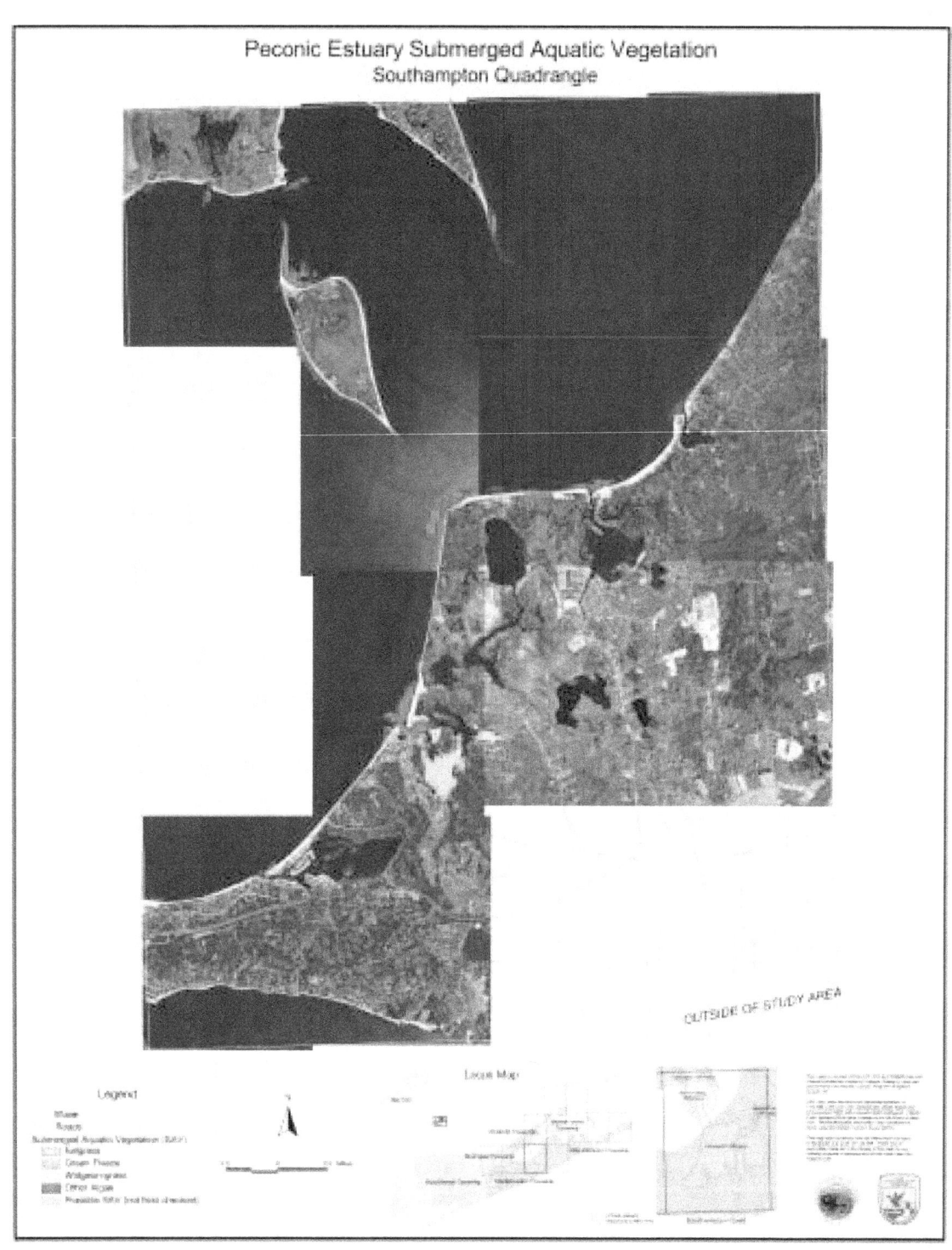

OUTSIDE OF STUDY AREA

Legend

Peconic Estuary Submerged Aquatic Vegetation
Southold Quadrangle

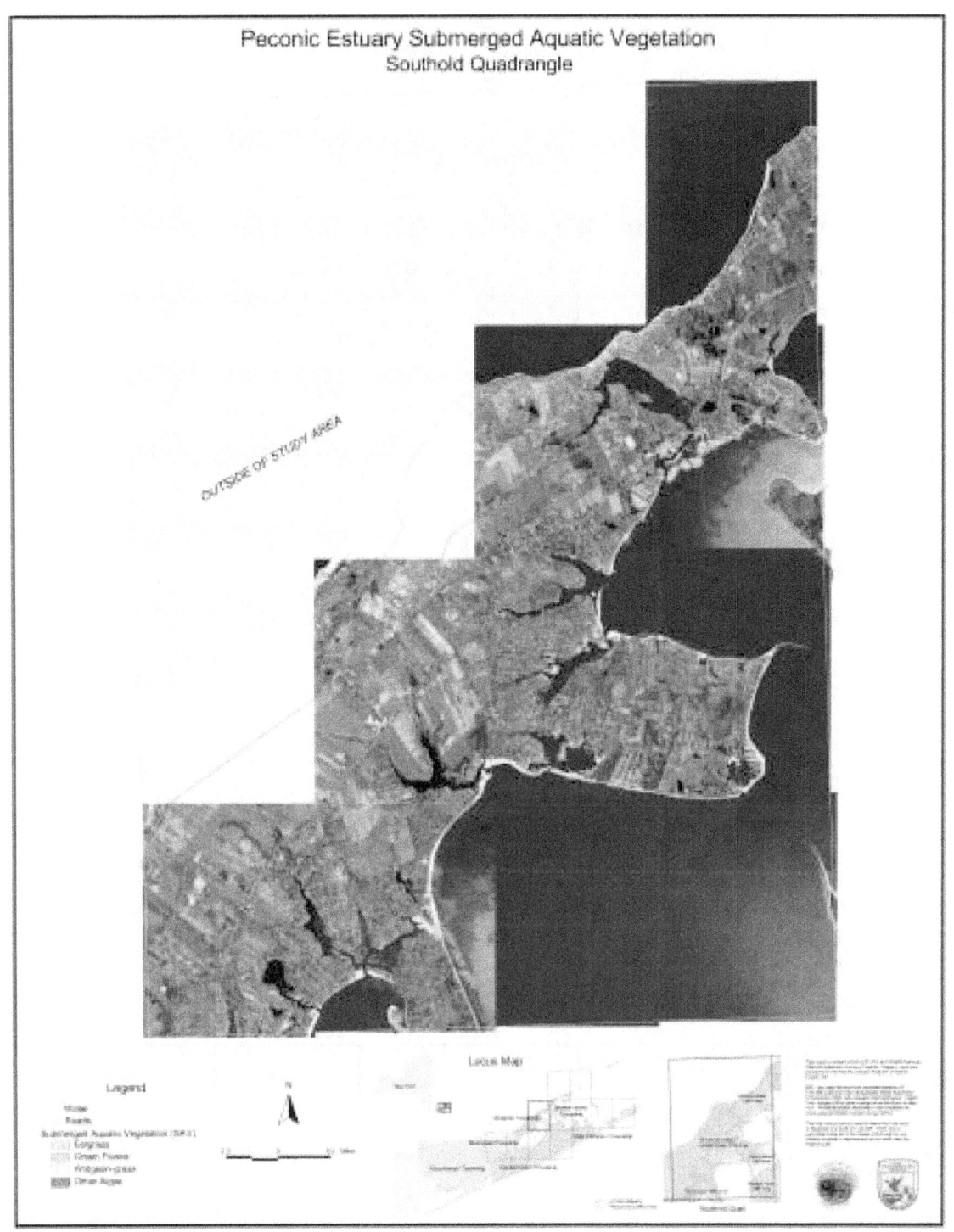

Appendix B.

Maps showing the extent of hardened shorelines and docks in the Peconic Estuary

(<u>Note</u>: The Gardiners Island East map includes part of the Napeague Beach quadrangle)

Peconic Estuary Hardened Shorelines
Gardiners Island East Quadrangle

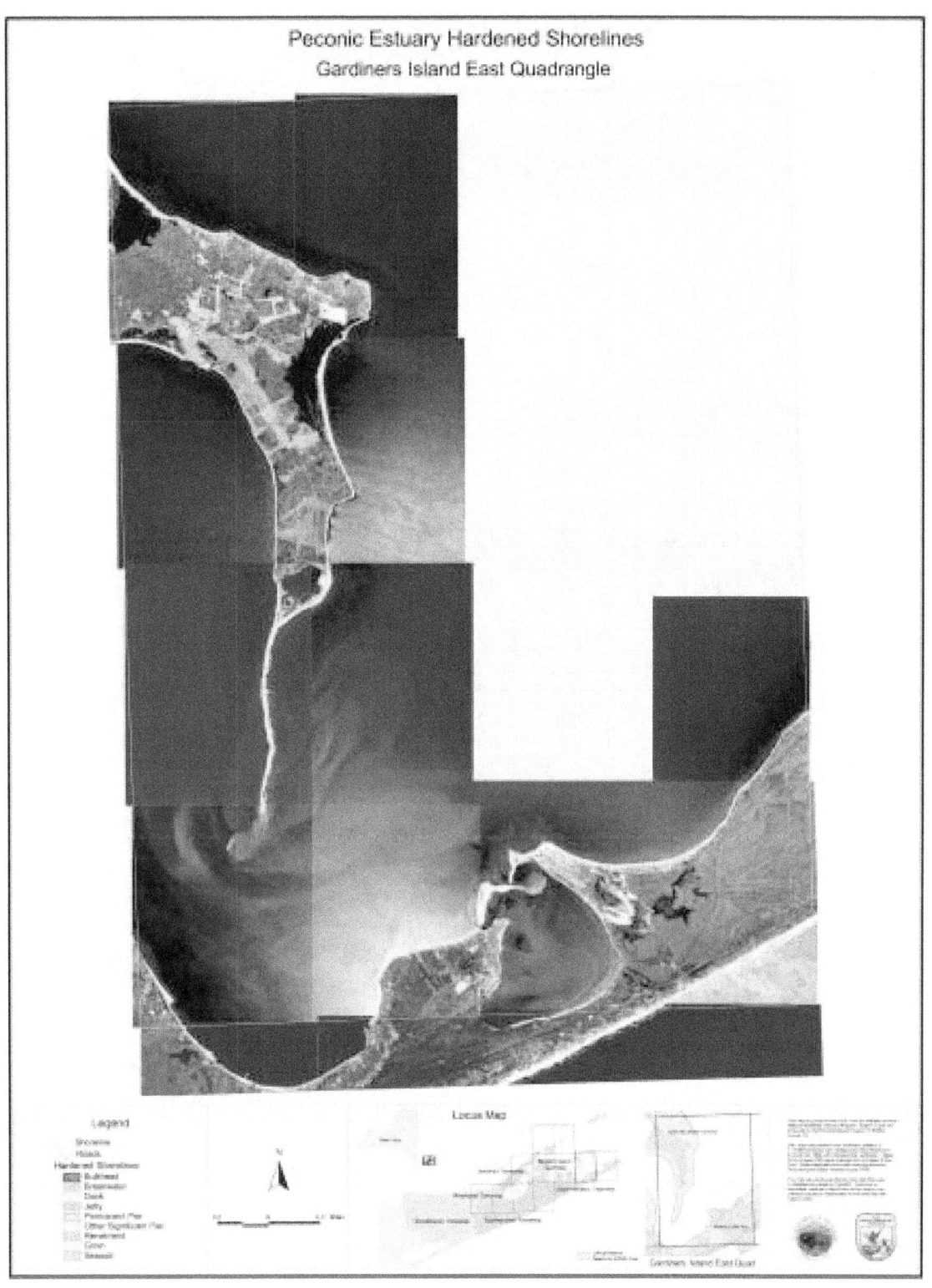

Peconic Estuary Hardened Shorelines
Gardiners Island West Quadrangle

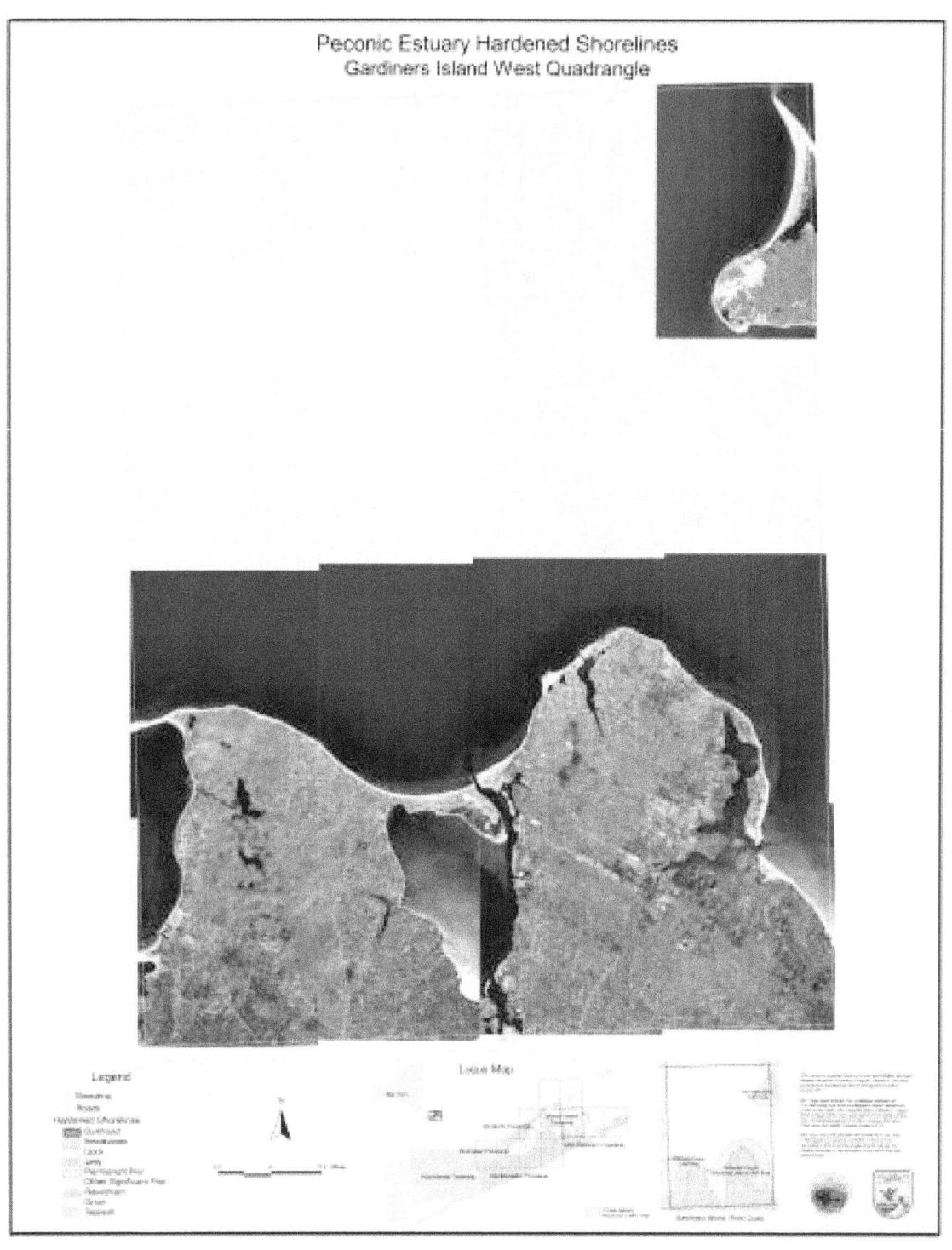

Peconic Estuary Hardened Shorelines
Greenport Quadrangle

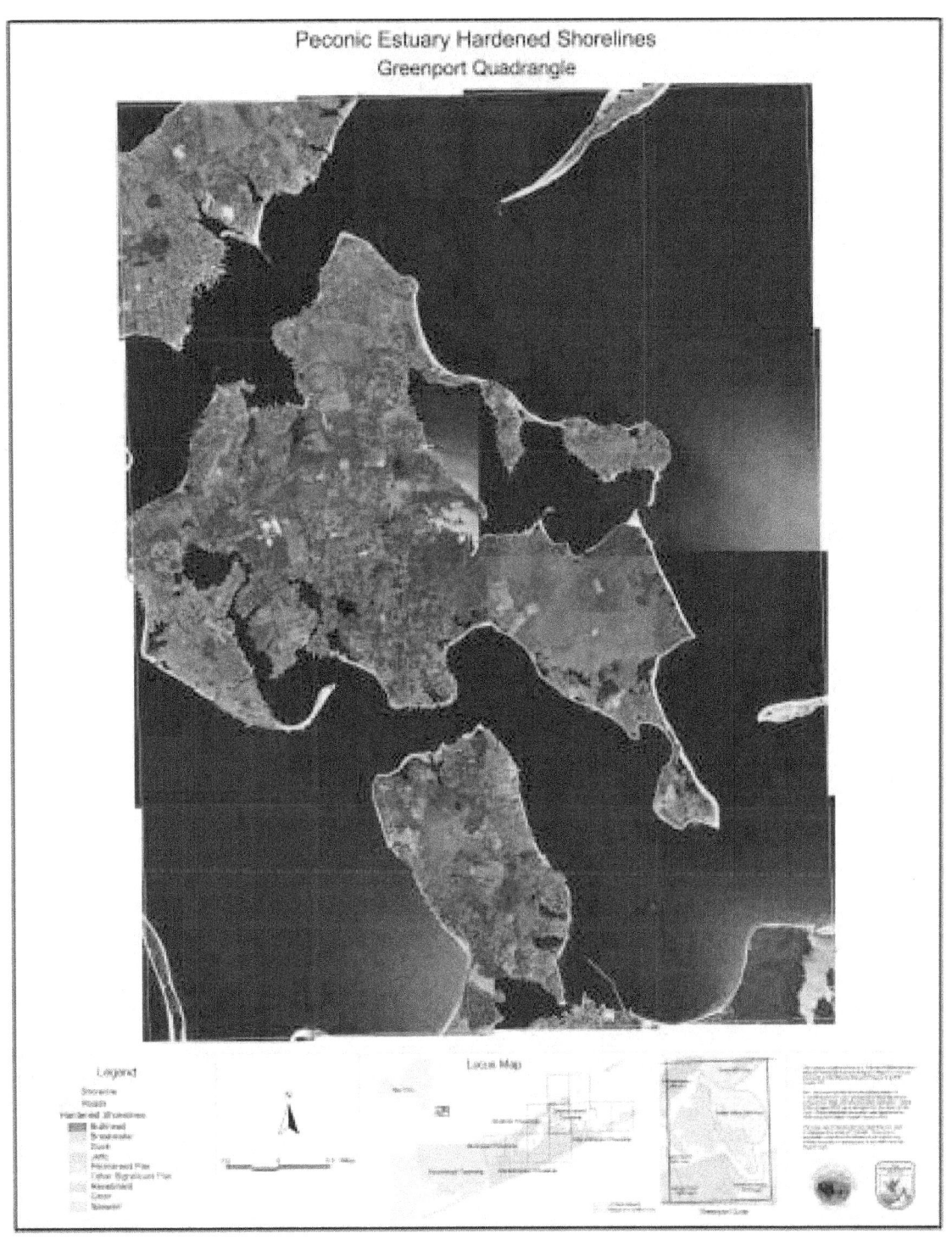

Legend

Shoreline

Roads

Hardened Shorelines

Locus Map

Peconic Estuary Hardened Shorelines
Mattituck Quadrangle

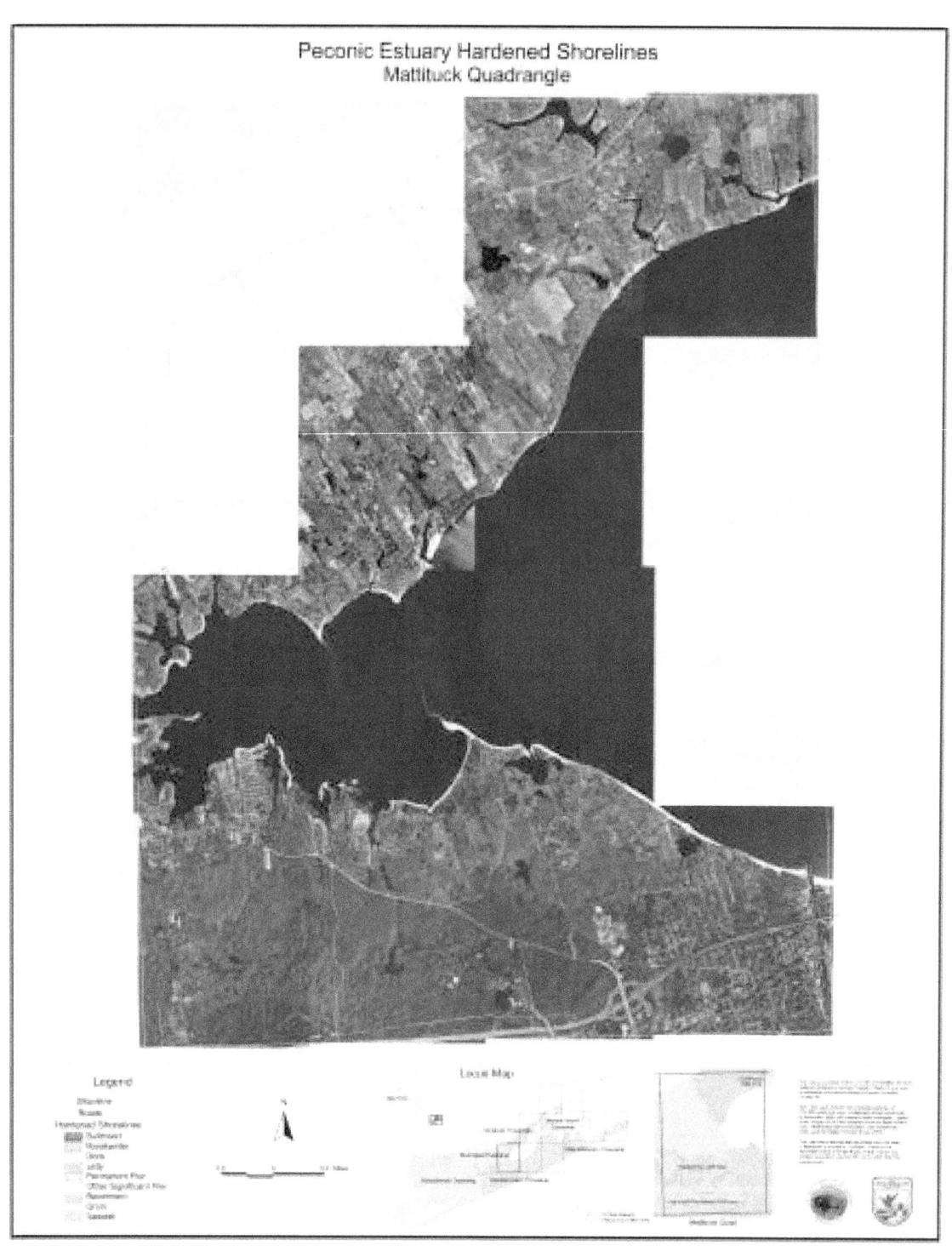

Peconic Estuary Hardened Shorelines
Montauk Point Quadrangle

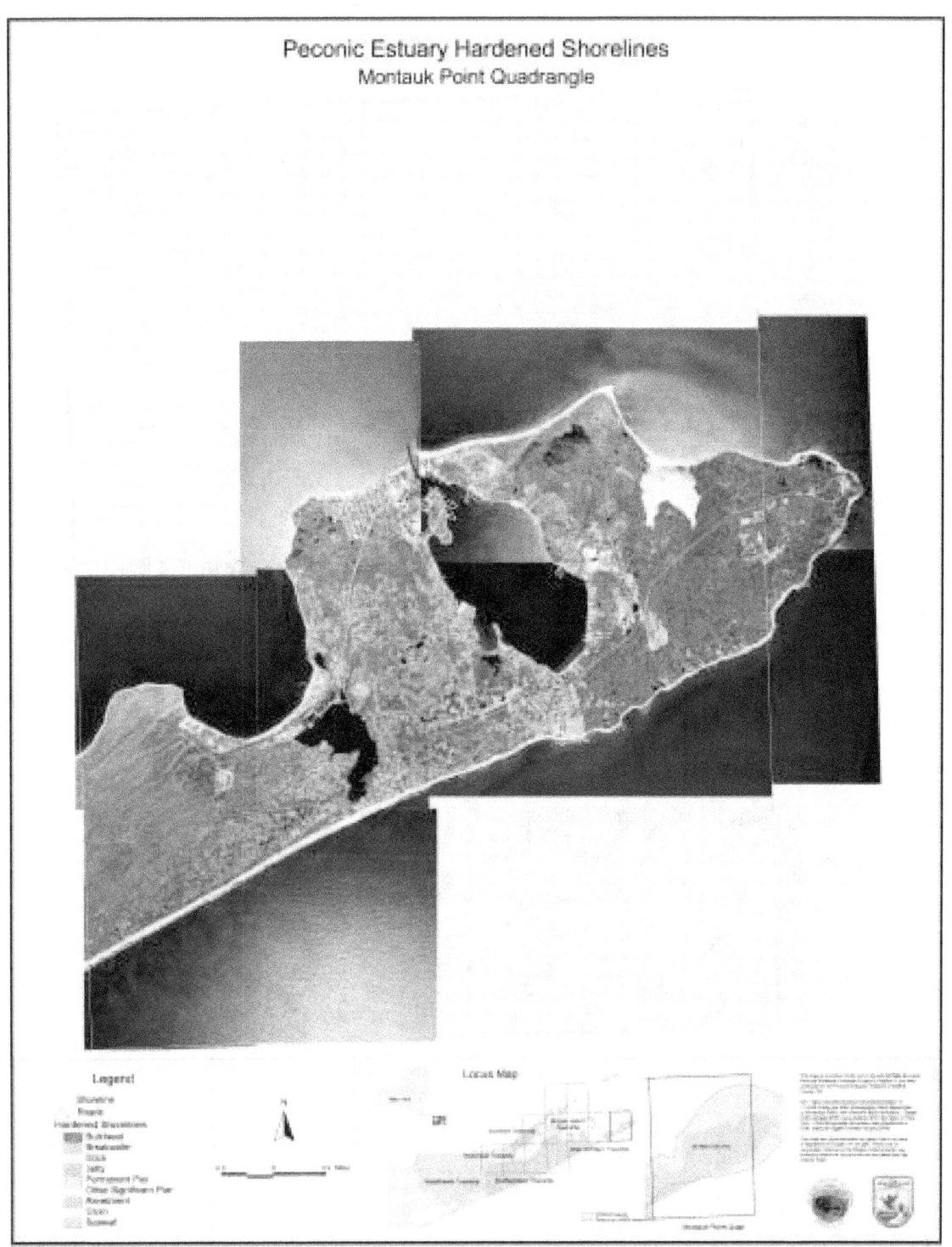

Peconic Estuary Hardened Shorelines
Orient Quadrangle

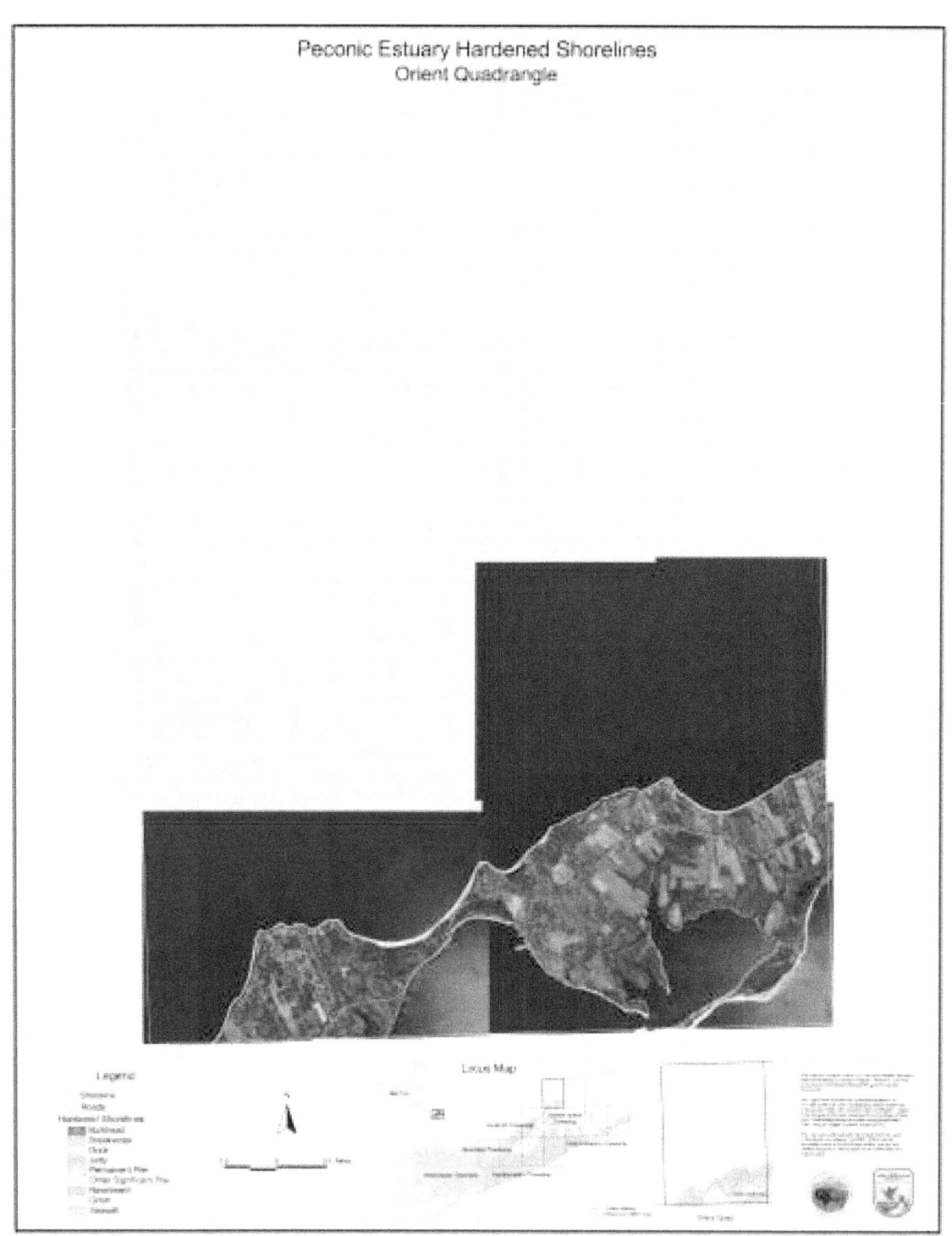

Peconic Estuary Hardened Shorelines
Plum Island Quadrangle

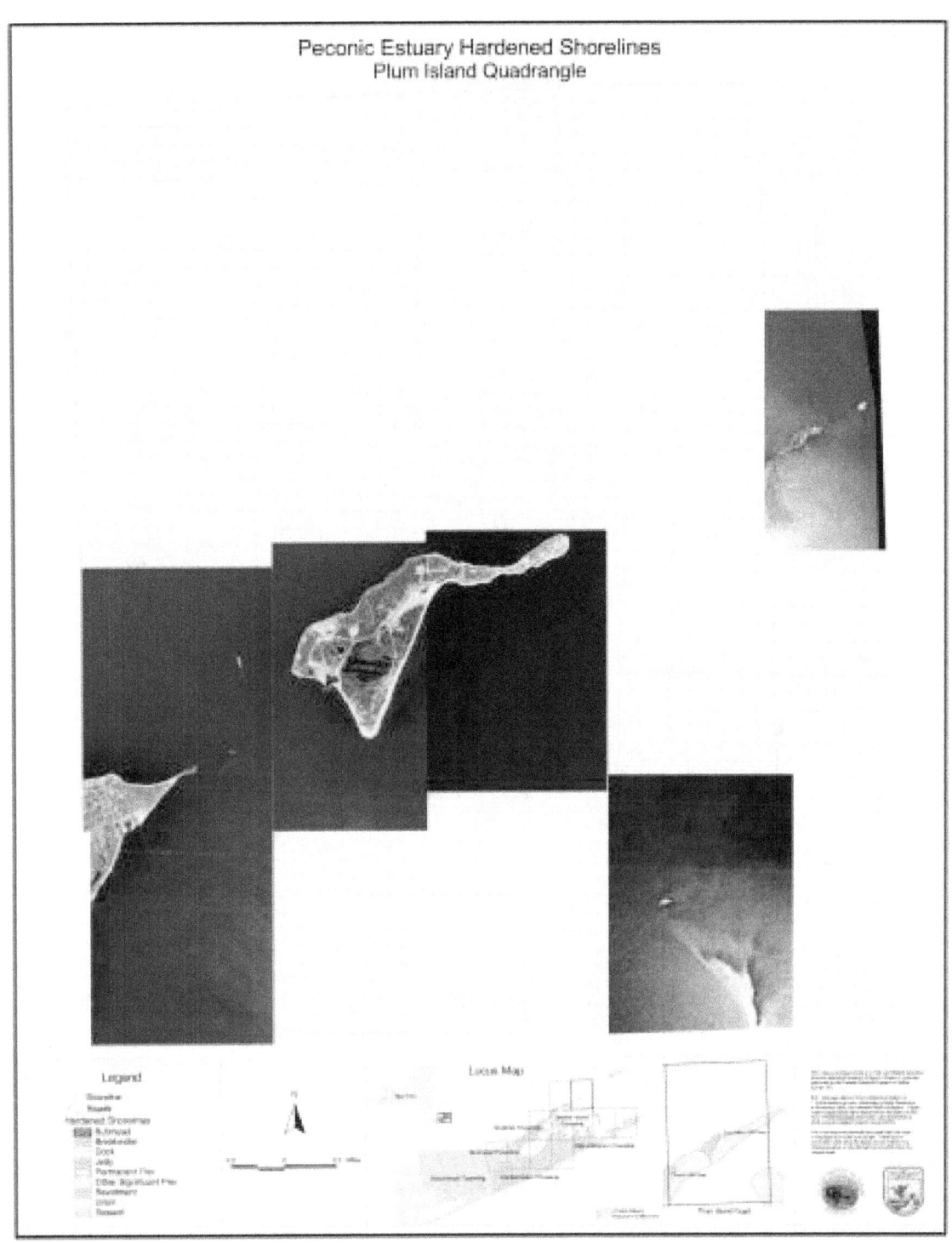

Peconic Estuary Hardened Shorelines
Riverhead Quadrangle

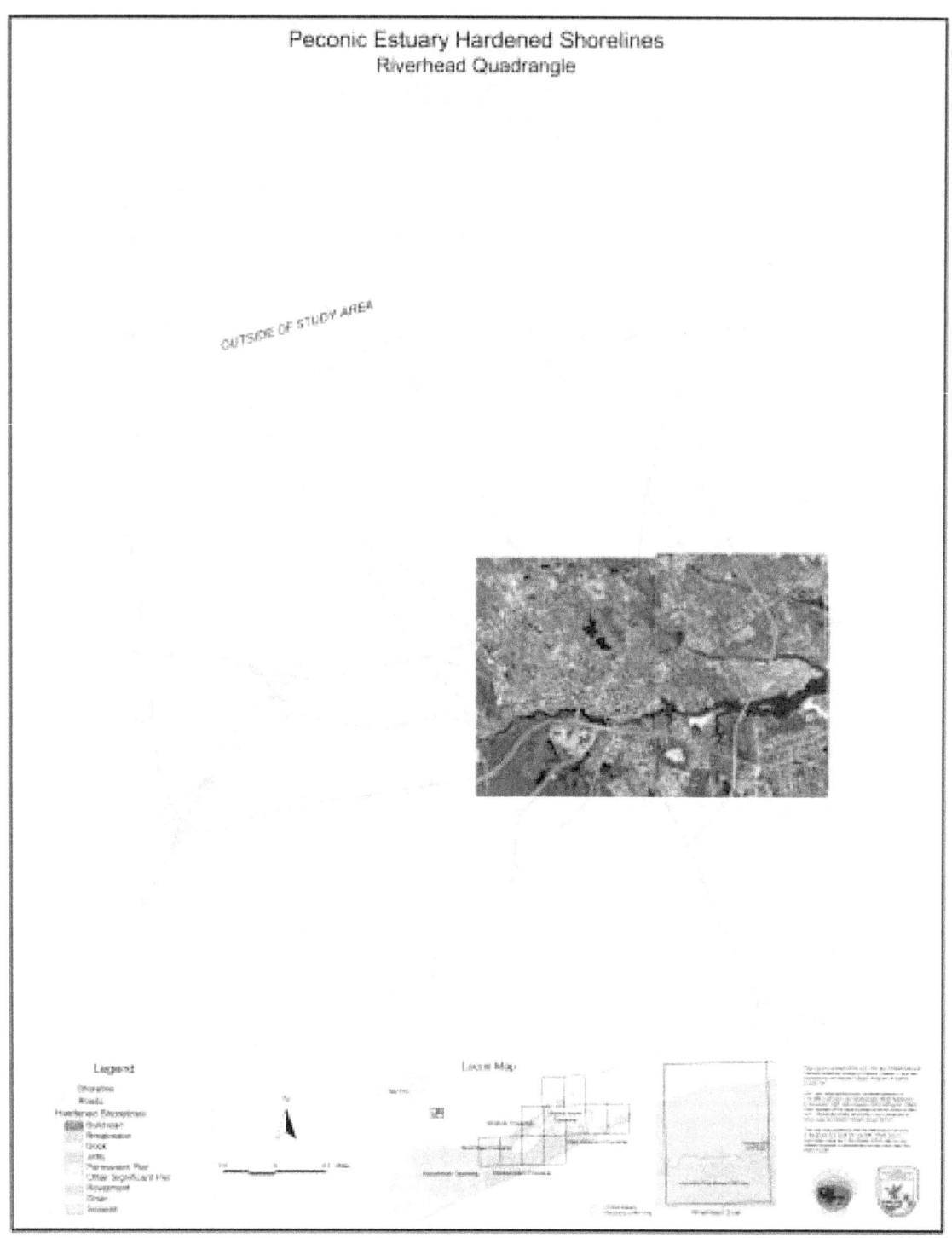

OUTSIDE OF STUDY AREA

Peconic Estuary Hardened Shorelines
Sag Harbor Quadrangle

OUTSIDE OF STUDY AREA

Legend

Locus Map

Peconic Estuary Hardened Shorelines
Southampton Quadrangle

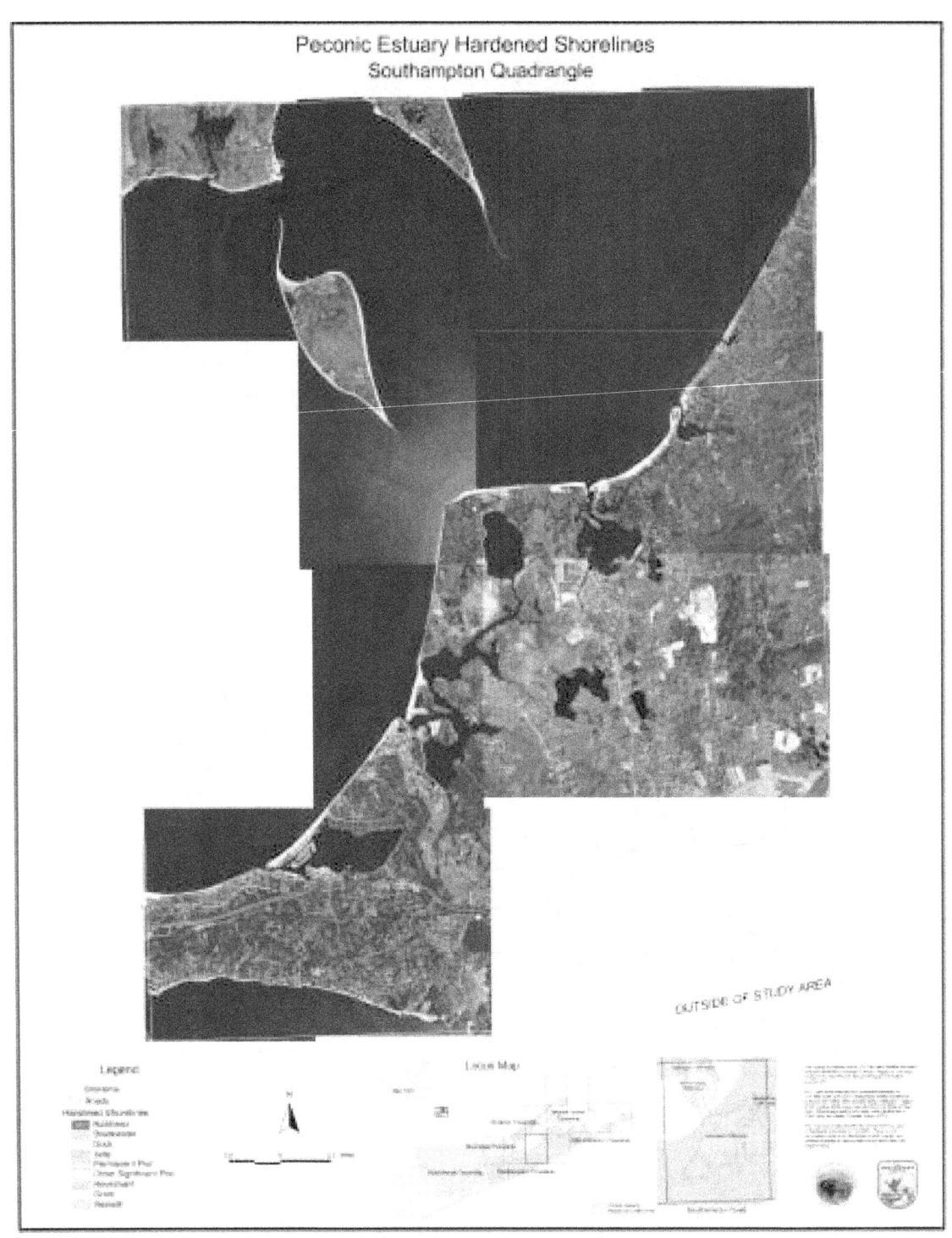

OUTSIDE OF STUDY AREA

Peconic Estuary Hardened Shorelines
Southold Quadrangle

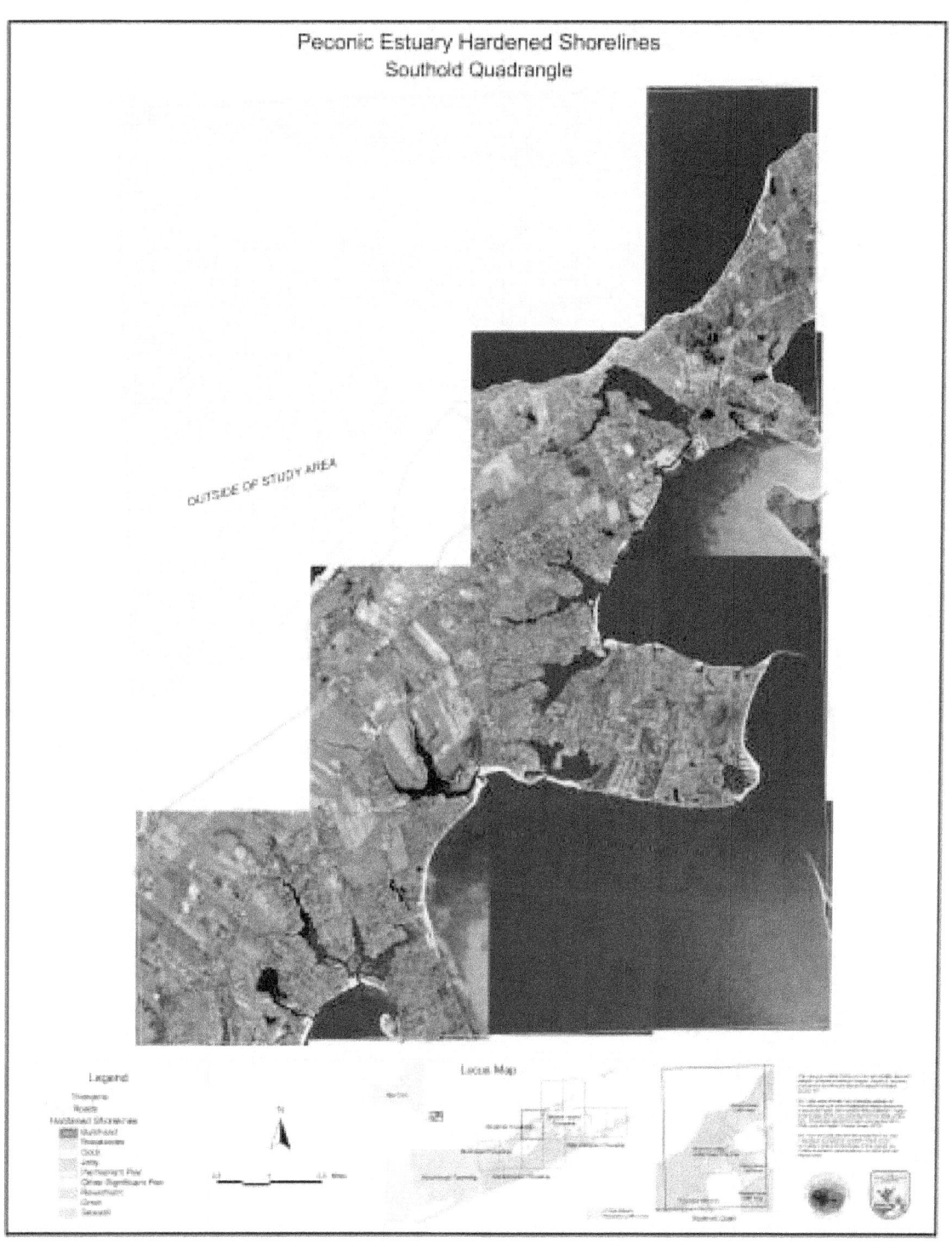

OUTSIDE OF STUDY AREA